Bootst
an
Biscuits

300 wonderful wild food recipes from the hills of West Virginia

Anna Lee Robe-Terry

ISBN 1-891852-14-0
(Formerly ISBN 0-87012-587-7)

Published by Quarrier Press
(Previously published by McClain Printing)

Library of Congress Catalog Card Number: 97-092831

Printed in the United States of America

12 11 10 9 8 7 6 5 4 3

Distributed by:
Pictorial Histories Distribution
1416 Quarrier Street
Charleston, WV 25301

ACKNOWLEDGMENTS

Many people have help me to get this book together and out to you. To each of them I am very grateful.

I especially want to thank Kim Rager and Charlene Morgan for typing that first draft (on the kitchen table); Janice Lake and Anna Ours for their proof-reading; Greg Eddy for checking out and correcting all the scientific names; Ann Payne for the cover; Mary Rodd Furbee for marketing and publication advise and assistance and finally the Appalachian Folklife Foundation, especially its President, Linda Cooper, for layout, technical assistance and much encouragement.

Thanks also to numerous family members and friends who have been supportive and helpful.

I am grateful also to be able to utilize the wonderful illustrations from Strausbaugh and Core's Flora of West Virginia and also to Jody Boyd and Ann Payne for additional illustrations.

To the memory of my mother and
my grandparents, who taught me to
use and appreciate the foraged foods,
and to my son, Douglas, who
encouraged me to write it all down,
I affectionately dedicate this book.

INTRODUCTION

In 1976, I found myself with a disabling illness. Pretty soon my job, home, car and furniture was all gone. I kept three pieces of jewelry that had a special meaning to me and they got stolen. My insurance company went bankrupt. I was left with nothing and sick to boot. My nursing career helped me in that department and my childhood experiences helped, too. I had a very small income. If the world gives you wild grapes you make jam and that is about what I did.

I moved in the milkhouse on my family's old farm, nothing fancy. Really it was little more than a shack, but it became home for me. I could not exercise but the doctor said walk a mile everyday. I began walking and I would find all this wild food. Remembering my childhood, I started gathering my food and working on ways to use it. I also gathered pretty flowers, grasses, etc., and used them to make gifts and decorations. If I found a plant I didn't know I tried to learn about it. I'm still learning new plants but I believe I have now learned all the trees growing about. I have also been able to learn about the wildlife that abounds around here. I still walk most everyday but it is becoming more difficult to make that mile. My book is finished now and for that I am glad because it seems my sense of taste and smell are going so I could not taste what I had developed.

I could not have done all this without the help of family, friends and neighbors. For them I am grateful. I cannot but help to think that the way of life has slowed this crippling disease down. Peace of mind and learning to except what I can't change has helped also. How long I will be able to continue I don't know but I do know I have inherited a stubborn will and know how to continue. My son and his friends were always tasting and asking questions about all these wild foods. They decided we should do a video of these plants and things. I really never felt it was that important and we never got around to it. Then when my son died it became very important to get this down on paper as I had no one to leave this knowledge to. Only a mother who has lost her only child will know how that affects you. Once again, I pulled myself up by my bootstraps and continued my life. This book is the results of that trauma. I hope many others will learn and perhaps use this information.

Anna Lee Robe-Terry
June 29, 1992

A WORD OF CAUTION:
This book is not a field guide for wild foods identification and is not intended for such use. If you need assistance identifying wild plants, please refer to an authoritative reference.

TABLE OF CONTENTS

Wild Salad Plants

There are so many wild salad plants. A complete book could be written just of them. None are available for year-round use, but the cress species of one kind or the other is almost year-round. The first cress will start growing in February in a cold winter. In mild winters, one can find the cresses and chickweed growing in any plowed ground.

A nice walk in the Spring, gathering greens either for salad or to cook, is a pleasant occupation for both body and soul. Take a basket and knife and go. Take only the part of the plant you will eat and leave the rest. This will make cleaning and washing much easier. I will list only a few here. The dressing for these salads is almost always a hot dressing, so as to wilt the leaves.

Hot Dressing for Wilted Salads

1 egg beaten	1/4 cup vinegar
1/4 cup sugar	1/4 cup water

A few strips of bacon fried crisp

Fry and crumble the bacon. Mix all ingredients and add to hot skillet stirring till thickened. Pour over the prepared salad greens. Add the bacon pieces. Serve.

If you don't find enough greens, the salad may be extended by the addition of garden lettuce. Please don't use iceberg lettuce as it is mostly water and does not wilt well. With the addition of a sliced onion, your salad is ready. With the rage of not using animal fat, it only takes a little modifying of the recipe. Use heated olive oil and add imitation bacon bits. Then, add the vinegar-sugar solution.

Amaranth
Amaranthus retroflexus

Wild Salad Plants:

Amaranth - Amaranthus retroflexus
Asparagus - Asparagus officinalis
Bramble - Rubus spp. - when very young
Bull Thistle - C. Pumilum - try peeling the stalk
Burdock - Arctium minus - young leaf and peeled stalk
Cattail - Typha latifolia - young shoots
Chickweed - Stellaria media
Cress - Cardamine spp.
Dandilion - Taraxacum offiande - bitter after blooming
Day lily - Hemerocallis fulva - young shoots
Dock - Rumex spp.

Bull Thistle
Cirsium pumilum

Burdock
Arctium minus

Wild Lettuce
Lactuca canadensis

Wild Salad Plants **continued**

Lamb's quarter - Chenopodium spp.
Peppergrass - Lepidium spp.
Plantain - Plantago major
Purslane - Portulaca oleracea
Queen Anne's lace - Daucus carota - carrot flavor
Sorrell - Rumex acetosella
Spiderwort - Tradescantia virginian
Watercress - Nasturtium officinale
Wild alliums - Allium spp.
Wild lettuces - Lactuca spp.
Wild Mustards - Brassica spp.
Winter Cress - Barbarea vulgaris
Yucca - Yucca filamentosa - use flowers

Plantain
Plantago major

Field Sorrel
Rumex acetosella

Wild Greens Quiche

3 eggs
2 tablespoons flour
1/4 cup chopped onion
3 slices of bacon fried
1/2 teaspoon savory
1 cup cooked drained greens
1/4 cup grated cheese
1/4 cup milk
1/2 cup water
1 9-inch unbaked pie shell

Beat eggs, flour, seasoning, add milk and water. Beat well. Place the greens, chopped onion and cheese in pie shell. Pour over the egg mixture. Top with the fried bacon that has been crumbled. Bake 350 degrees for 35 minutes.

Wild Greens Souffle

2 cups cooked and drained greens
1/4 cup Parmesan cheese
1/8 teaspoon cream of tartar
2 eggs separated
Salt / pepper

To the cooked greens, add the beaten egg yolks. Place in double boiler and cook until the eggs are firm. Cool. Sprinkle with Parmesan cheese and break up with a fork. Set oven on 350 degrees and place in a pan of hot water. Beat egg whites with 1/8 teaspoon of cream of tartar. Fold the whites into the egg-greens mixture. Spray 4 individual serving dishes with Pam. Fill 1/2 full with the mixture and place in the pan of water in the oven. Bake for 30 minutes and serve immediately or they will fall.

Pot Herbs

Going green picking is a nice pleasant walk in the woods, fields, yard, barn yard and will produce a nice supper any day. Springtime is the best as most greens get tough as the summer comes along. Encourage your friends and family to come with you so they can learn all of the plants. Where would I have been if my mother and grandparents had not made the effort to teach me?

I am sure these foods will be lost soon if we don't continue passing along our heritage. West Virginians are a hardy bunch and maybe eating so much of these wild foods has kept them that way. The work or exercise that it takes to gather and clean these has it benefits too. In picking these wild foods, take a basket and a sharp knife. Find what there is and clean the spent stems or leaves and roots, leaving to compost and fertilize the next crop. Never, never pick all of any one plant. Always leave some for seed.

Black Mustard
Brassaca nigera

You will need to separate the plants that need parboiled from the others that only need to be cooked once. Remember that a whole bucket of greens will be reduced by 2/3s or more after cooking. After the greens are parboiled, combine them with the others and have ready a hot iron skillet with a lump of pork fat. Gently stew, and fix a big pan of corn bread, some milk and maybe a few salt-water cooked potatoes . . . and. . . supper is ready.

Salt water potatoes are just peeled potatoes cooked in salt water. The water can then be boiled and reduced in half and used to make maple-like syrup. To each cup (strained) of this water, heat and stir in 1 cup of white and 1 cup of brown sugar. If that meal won't build a healthy body, nothing will! Medical authorities know that West Virginians have a higher red blood count than other folks. They say it is from using iron skillets and pans. As far as I'm concerned, they can keep most of the other cookware, however, I do use stainless steel. A Teflon skillet is not fit to hang in my cupboard.

I can usually start picking greens in February or March. I will start with the first and follow into others.

Wild Allium--see Allium chapter
Blackberry - Rubus spp.- young stalks and leaves
Chickweeds - Stellaria spp.
Clover - Trifolium spp.
Comfrey - Symphytum officinale
Dandelion leaves - see Tea and Coffee Substitutes section
Dock - Rumex crispus
Field Sorrel - Rumex spp.
Greenbriers (Blaspheme-vine) - Smilax spp.
Horseradish - Armoracia lapathifolia -in limited quantity and only young leaves
Japanese Knotweed - polygonum cuspidatum
Lamb's quarter - Chenopodium album
Milkweed - Asclepias syriaca
Wild Mustards - Brassica spp.
Nettle - Urtich dioica
Plantain - Plantago spp.
Poke - Phytolacca americana
Purslane - Portulaca oleracea
Prickly and Wild Lettuce - Lactuca spp.
Shepherd's purse - Capsella bursa-pastoris
Spring cress - Barbarea verna
Violets - Viola spp.- both leaf and flower
Wood Sorrels - Oxalis spp.

Red Clover
Trifolium pratense

Pot Herbs continued

Garden Rocket - Erucastrum gallicum - better known elsewhere as the Winter Field Watercress
"Winter" cress - Cardamine pensylvanica- or Pennsylvania bittercress

Garden Rocket
Erucastrum gallicum

Comfrey
Symphytum officinale

These wild plants are known by many names, each familiar in specific areas. This list of wilds will be usable till your garden is ready and that is the reason these have been passed down all these years. There are other wild foods coming along till winter. Nor have I named all that can be gathered. I am sure that you know others. In my range, these are available to me and used.

Greenbrier
Smilax rotundifolia

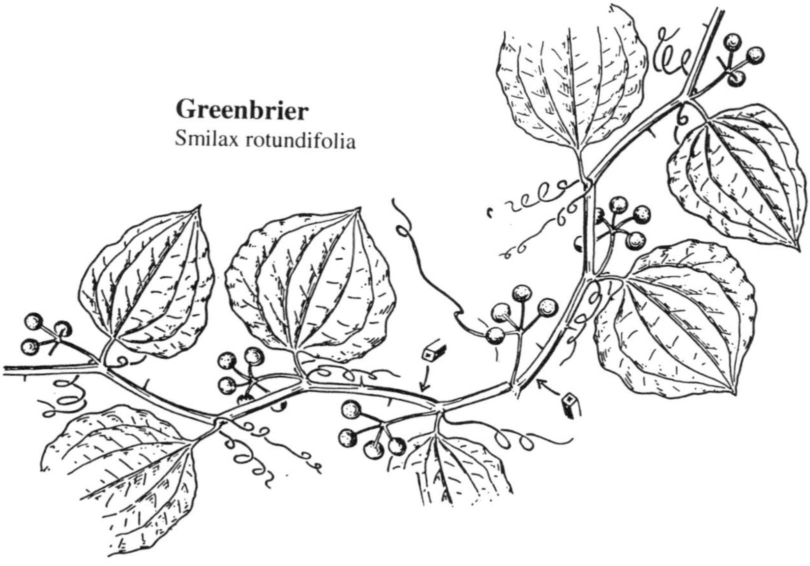

Wild Seasonings

If you need a seasoning, there are several you can forage from the wilds instead of from the grocer's shelf. Some you will not like but, some I like better. Spicewood berries are one of these. I can't imagine making the wild grape sauce without it. The flavors will not be the same as the cultivated ones but only slightly different. In some cases, you will need to use more but not usually less. The wild ginger is like this. You need to use more wild ginger to achieve the ginger flavor in a recipe calling for ginger. Unless you have oodles of this, please don't dig it up from the wild. If you have a large patch, take care of it so it won't disappear. Check your State laws to make sure the plants you are harvesting are not on the endangered species list. Wild ginger (aristolochiaceae) is a native plant used by the Indians and is not related to commercial ginger. If you want to try cultivating it, plant in rich soil and in the shade. In cold climates, you cannot grow regular ginger but you might have good luck with the wild ginger. If all else fails, purchase the ginger roots at the local grocery store.

Listed below are taste alikes:

1. Horseradish like taste--spring cress; toothwort
2. Sour taste--sheep sorrel (raw only)
3. Salt--burned coltsfoot, powdered
4. Caraway--Wild caraway seeds like the cultivated kind
5. Licorice--Angelica stems; sweet golden rod
6. Onion--garlic; leeks (see chapter on these)
7. Vanilla--white sweet clover leaves
8. Mustard--wild mustard; winter crest seeds
9. Mint--several mints can be found
10. Pepper like--Cow Cress; Shepherds Purse;
    Field pennycress; poor man's pepper
11. Basil--wild basil
12. Allspice--spicewood
13. Juniper berries -Rosemary / tarragon like flavor
14. Thyme--green sassafras leaves

Tea and Coffee Substitutes

Mother Nature's cupboard is full of teas, that are really good as well as good for you. I would really be hard put to choose the one I like the best. They are, each in their own time, the best. Some can be dried for all-year use, but some are just for now and then they are gone. The green mints are a good example. No dried mint will taste like a green one, and only in the growing season can you have the green mint. Sumac is good for only about one month and for that month, it is my favorite. Then again, on a cold blustery winter day, nothing can take the place of a cup of sassafras tea.

Cold water mint teas are made by placing the fresh plant (about one cup) in a blender of cold water. Blend or chop briefly and let set for thirty minutes, or longer. This will let the flavor come out into the water from your plant. Strain and adjust to suit your taste. Add sweetener of your choice. I keep a bottle of simple syrup in the refrigerator. I make this syrup by cooking 2 cups of sugar with one cup water, stirring till sugar is melted. There are several types of mint growing wild or you can help it out by transplanting your favorite near you. Next year, you won't be sorry.

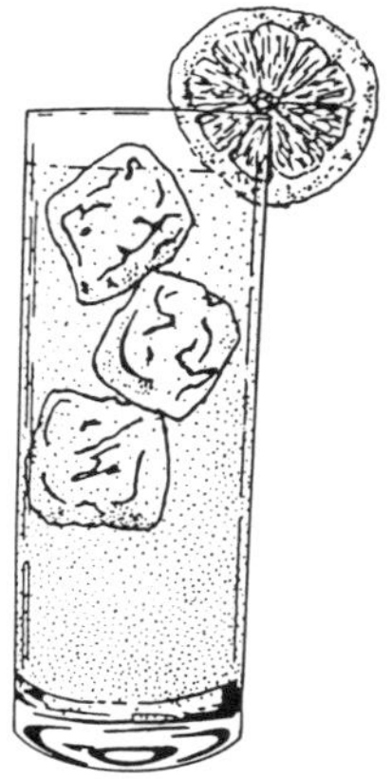

In a good year, I will cut the mints about 3 times. In average years, I cut twice. If it is really dry, I pick very limited.

I do gather a lot of herbs. Peppermint, spearmint, and mountain mint all are a little different in taste. I save the elastic from panty hose tops to help with bundling these for drying. Wrap the elastic around the stems and pull the other end through. Now hang on your walking stick. I can pick several different kinds and they are ready to hang to dry when I get home. So, when you go gathering, be prepared. You will soon know where something you want to find is growing. Usually, the plants will return year after year.

Never, never pick all the plants or destroy any of them. Make sure you have properly identified the plants. Label all these bunches because when they dry, they will all look alike. Hang to dry in an attic or similar place. Pick off when dry like some nice cold winter day. I keep my herb pan by the telephone and make tea bags while wasting time talking on the phone . . . and here's how.

My tea pot holds about a quart of water. I put it on to heat and when it comes to a boil, I put a tea bag in, turn off the heat and let it steep. I use honey or syrup to sweeten, and in some teas, I don't use anything. You will soon learn how much water and sugar you like for each mint you use.

I also gather other plants for hot teas. The berry leaves are all good--bee balm, catnip, camomile and cultivated herbs. All can be stored for winter. There are also herbs I gather for my own medical use, but I get to that later.

Coffee Filter Tea Bag

Take a coffee filter in your left hand and a hand full of your tea leaves in your right. Place in the coffee filter and bring all of the edges up together and tie close. You can color code these different teas. I usually use a recycled three pound coffee can to store the bags in. Labels can be added so you will always know what you have. They are safe from moisture and insects. The only better way would be glass jars, and they are a better choice for long storage, but I use mine up quickly.

The Teas I gather and dry for my own use:

Peppermint - Mentha piperita
Spearmint - Mentha spicata
Bee Balm - Monarda spp.
Horehound - Marrubium vulgare
Mullen - Verbascum thapsus
(Great Mullein)
Coltsfoot - Tussilago farfara
Comfrey- Symphytum officinale
Catnip - Nepeta cataria
Elderflower- Sambucus canadensis
(or Elderberry flower)
Camomile - Anthemis arvensis
(field chamomile)
Rose - Rosa carolina
Spicebush - Lindera benzoin

Chamomile
Anthemis arvens

Spicebush
Lindera benzoin

Pennyroyal - Hedeoma pulegioides (American pennyroyal) and Mentha pulegium (European pennyroyal)
Sassafras - Sassafras albidum
Raspberry Leaves - Rubus illecebrosus.
Blackberry root or leaf - Rubus spp.
Strawberry Leaves - Fragaria spp.
Ginger root - Asarum canadense

Bee Balm
Monarda didyma

Strong Plant Tea Basic Recipe

1 cup well-packed fresh leaf or flower of choice

3 cups water

Bring water to boil. Add the plant material. Remove from heat, cover and let steep. Strain. Add enough water to make 3 cups of tea.

Coffee-like Brews

Dandelion root, gathered, washed, dried, roasted to a dark brown, and ground.

Acorns can be used, but mostly the squirrels get these.

Yellow Goat's Beard -Tragopogon pratensis--roasted roots make a nice substitute for coffee.

Yellow Goat's Beard
Tragopogon pratensis

Common sunflower - Helianthus spp.- the hulls of the seeds can be roasted for a coffee-like substitute.

Chickory -Cichorium intybus- done the same as the dandelion. I prefer the dandelion and I have plenty of that growing the year around.

Goosegrass or Cleavers - Galium aparine--gather the ripe fruit, roast and grind for a really good coffee substitute.

Chufa - Cyperus esculentus--a nut grass growing in various places - the roots end in a nutlike tuber that is roasted, ground and made by boiling into coffee-like brew.

Cleavers/Goose grass
Galium aparine

Wild Mints

In addition to making teas with wild mints, as noted above, there are other ways to use wild mints. Here are a couple of my favorites:

Peppermint
Mentha piperita

Wild Mint Jelly

Gather about five pounds of wild yellow or green apples. Wash and cut apples. Place in the kettle and cover with water. Simmer till tender. Drain off the apple juice and measure. Return juice to boil, and reduce until you have 5 cups of concentrated juice. To this, add 2 cups concentrated mint juice made with 2 cups (any kind) mint leaves and 1 cup boiling water that you have let set to steep for thirty minutes. Strain. Measure liquids to equal 7 cups. Place in large jelly kettle and stir in 1 package of powdered pectin. Bring to a full rolling boil. Have ready 9 cups white sugar and pour all in slowly stirring. Bring back to a full boil, stirring for 1 minute. Remove from heat. Add a few drops of green food coloring and stir well. Remove foam. Pour into your hot sterilized jars. Seal. Place in a hot water bath and boil 10 minutes. A washed and dried mint leaf can be added to the jar, if you like.

Wild Mint Sorbet

One cup fresh mint leaves whizzed in the blender, with 2 cups of cold water. Let set, strain, make sure you have 2 full cups of tea mix for 2 cups of white sugar. Heat to melt. Add juice and zest of one lemon. Let cool. Place in freezer tray till frozen mushy, about one hour. Beat up the sorbet with a fork. Beat one egg white and fold in the mint mixture. Return to the freezer. Freeze till firm. Break up with fork, beat and place in pretty glasses. Decorate with a mint sprig and lemon peel.

Basic Jelly and Jam

Most edible plants or flowers can be made into jelly. If using herbs such as basil, mint, sage, oregano, etc., they are usually served with meats. The flower jellies can be used for glazes and decorations as well as on waffles and toast.

Basic Recipe for Plant Jelly / Jam

3 cups plant, tea-strong	4 cups sugar
3 tablespoons vinegar	1 teaspoon oil
1 box powdered pectin	

Place tea in jelly kettle, add vinegar, oil and pectin. Bring to a boil. Add sugar slowly but all at once. Stir and return to a hard boil. Stir and boil one minute. Place in sterilized glass jars. Refrigerate or can in hot water bath.

If you want jams, use the leaf or flower without straining out. Try using ramps, wild onion or garlic for a different jam to go with meats.

The Wild Allium Family

Wild Onion (Allium cernuum) looks just like wild garlic but blooms.

Wild Onion
Allium cernuum

Wild Garlic (Allium canadense) has tiny bulblets on the top. I use whatever I find in any place I need an onion flavor and keep some growing near the kitchen door. You can usually find them growing the year around, but when the grass and other flora are growing and are high, I have no time to go hunt my wild onions. In the winter and spring, they will pull easily, but come summer when you pull all you get is the top. In the summer, I usually resort to just the top bulbs, if I find a patch. These can be used as well and are dried to keep on hand. The tops are cooked with the early pot herbs and, some times, I gather the root bulbs for a nice dish of creamed onions on toast or cornbread.

Wild Garlic
Allium canadense

My poor Grandpa George must be turning over in his grave to think I would plant or even consider having a wild onion on the place. You see, he kept milk cows and sold cream, cheese and butter The wild onions were a real problem for him as they ruined his milk products if the cow ate them. So, over the whole farm, he destroyed all the wild onion by grubbing them out, at times by the light of a lantern, ai burning them on a brush pile. Even then, some of them lived and he had to re-do the whole operation. I remember one time coming home from school and finding some. I pulled them and brought them home to find o what I had. Well, my father, in a very stern voice, told me what I had an I was instructed to not lose a one and to put them back where I found them, 'cause he was following the same footsteps as his father on the sar farm. Wild onions were for the devil's workshop, not his farm. I still liv on that farm, but it is no longer a farm. It has been divided and now has the seventh generation living here and plenty of wild garlic, onion and a few ramps.

If you pull a bulb or pick something you think is from the allium family, just sniff it and you will know for sure. If it does not smell like onion, garlic or leek, let it stay there. Chances are it's not to be eaten.

In our family, the tradition of eating wild food and game is still going on. It's a way of life and I hope it will always be passed down in years to come. However, some is lost each generation, I am sorry to say. Our forefathers and mothers knew these foods, as well as medicines, and all about the different trees and what use each was best for. We are losing this.

The Wild Allium Family continued

Ramps are really wild leek (Allium tricoccum). A true ramp lover will add them to most anything s/he may fancy but most especially raw. They are such a delicacy for such a short time each spring. However, they can be enjoyed year-round by freezing and some folks can them also.

To Freeze—clean and blanch ramps. Drain. Place a few in a plastic sandwich bag. Wrap in freezer paper and place loosely in a wide mouth glass jar and turn top down tightly. You can remove a package at any time of the year. These must be stored in a glass jar or the odor will be all over the other foods in your freezer. Ramps have a very potent odor. It will linger on your body and breath for quite some time—days, in fact. Eating parsley raw and brushing your teeth with baking soda will help dispel the odor. Cutting boards, knives, etc., can be placed in a vinegar wash to rid them of odor. That little bulb that looks like a lily is loved by many and hated by some.

Ramp/Wild Leek
Allium tricoccum

Pickled Ramps

Clean a quantity of ramps. I like to cut off the tops and freeze those. The white bulb part is then added to equal parts sugar and vinegar. Heat while stirring. Place in a jar. Seal. Place in refrigerator about two weeks. If you are making more than 1 jar, you will need to process in a hot water bath for 10 minutes.

Wild Garlic Butter

½ lb. unsalted butter
1 tablespoon parsley
3 tablespoons wild garlic, onion or leek

Let butter soften at room temperature. Chop parsley. Mash garlic cloves. Mix well. Cover.

Day Lily (Hemerocallis fulva) can be found growing along roads, in meadows and almost anywhere in the Northeastern United States. Several varieties are edible but this is the one I have. The whole plant is used. The roots, tiny bulbs, are dug when the plant is dormant. You will not harm the plant as this acts like cultivating and spreads the bulb further. The young shoots are also eaten in salads and cooked with pot herbs or alone. Later when the flower buds appear they can be harvested and when the flowers bloom they are also utilized. All these many foods from just one plant! Always be sure to leave some of this lily when harvesting in any of the stages you use it.

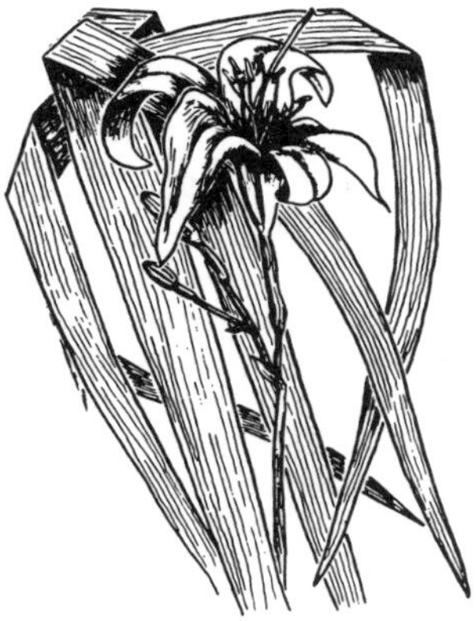

Day Lily
Hemerocallis fulva

Day Lily Shoots

Harvest, wash and cook in any way you would asparagus. You can extend your asparagus with these, if needed.

Unopened Day Lily Buds

Harvest these while green and before you can see any hint of orange. They will be well sealed this way and they remind me of young tender green beans. Place in a bit of boiling salted water and cook only about 5 minutes. Add a bit of butter and a sprinkle of summer savory, if you like.

Day Lily Blossom Fritters

Harvest the flower when just opening. Have the skillet hot and batter prepared then pick your blossoms. Dust flowers with flour. Dip in a thin batter and fry. Leftover pancake batter, thinned, is often used for this.

Day Lily Blossom Soup

The bloom only lasts one day so the next day pick the wilted blossoms and dry them for the following soup. They need to be shredded before or after drying. They can be added to other broths and soups as well. Add 5 dried blossoms to 4 cups heated chicken broth--heat but don't boil. Salt or butter is not really needed but can be added. Just before pouring into serving bowls, add about 1/4 teaspoon Oriental Five-Spice Blend. You should use less of this seasoning instead of more. I found it took some getting used to but the soup is not good without it. Garnish with sliced scallions.

Horseradish (Armoracia lapathifolia) is not a wild plant but in places it has escaped cultivation and is now growing wild about old homesteads. It requires little or no attention. Once it is established, it needs to be harvested just to keep it in bounds. The roots go underground 10 plus feet in every direction and it can just keep on growing. I dig it spring or fall or mostly when I need it. I aim for 1/2 of 1 plant when digging. A little bit goes a long way. I take the center clump when digging, the feeder roots will then become plants. Do not harvest the plant again for at least a year.

Cut the top inch off this root and re-plant. It will grow and you will have a plant handy all of the time. It really is a pretty plant too.

Horseradish
Armoracia lapathifolia

Scrub your root with a stiff brush, cut off the top and peel. I chop this root into small pieces, place it into a blender or chop. Do a small amount at a time. Add more pieces and white vinegar when needed. Pack the horseradish into a jar and make sure the vinegar covers it. I make it in small batches, because when exposed to air, it will lose its strength and discolor. Blenders are not all alike, so make sure yours is heavy duty enough for this job. You may find a food processor better. If all else fails, grate it like Grandma did on her grater. The root is very tough and fibrous. The oils are difficult to breathe, something akin to an onion. Do your grinding in a well ventilated area and your work will all be worth it. Horseradish plain or in a sauce is perfect accompaniment to meats and fish. Don't over look the young leaves for pot herbs or on a sandwich instead of lettuce.

Horseradish Cream Sauce for Meat

Mix 1 cup sour cream with 1 cup ground drained horseradish. Serve this with meat, especially roast beef.

Horseradish Sandwich Spread

Mix 1 cup mayonnaise with 1/2 cup grated, drained horseradish and 1/2 cup of grated carrots or turnips. Try this as a vegetable dip, too.

Ketchup and Horseradish Sauce

Mix equal parts of ketchup, horseradish, the juice and zest of 1 lemon. Try this with eggs and vegetables. We especially like this with fried potatoes and turnips. A nice way to introduce the younger folks to horseradish.

Horseradish Sauce for Fish

Mix 1 cup tomato paste with 1/2 c fresh grated horseradish. If too thick, add a bit of lemon juice to get it to consistency you want. Add 1 teaspoon sugar and 1/2 teaspoon salt. This sauce is made without vinegar and should be freshly grated as needed

Nettles (Urtich dioica) is not native to the United States of America. It was brought from Europe by a person or persons unknown. Due to its large protein, vitamin A, and C and trace mineral content, it is valued as food, medicine, yellow dye, fiber for making clothing, and animal feed. To be an animal feed, it must be dried, to avoid the stinging sensation which one gets when skin comes into contact with it. When the nettle comes into contact with the bare skin, it is very painful. Each tiny hairy profusion of the plant is full of a venom, called formic acid. Normally this plant is contacted while walking in a wooded area. It grows in clumps or patches in rich damp areas of the forest. Also found in this area are the first aid remedies of dock and jewel weed. To apply this, crush the stems and rub the juices over the skin. The soothing action of these plants, will soon drive the pain away. The use of this plant, as either a food, medicine, dye, or fiber is hard to believe. However, after its use, you will be converted.

Stinging Nettles
Urtich dioica

Just wash it, cook and salt to taste, to make delicious greens. It can be used in omelets, after being cooked, and I personally like it in Chicken and Dumplings. Grandma always used an old fat hen, cooking it until well done, then putting nettle greens and noodles in the chicken broth to cook. Grandma said, nettles for supper, and Grandpa is going to fuss. He detested the things and said that they should go back to the devil, where they belonged. As a cooked green, it just can't be beat. I notice the deer browse the tender tops. Dried for tea I really don't care for it. There are so many other teas I like better. I have not tried it as an appetite suppressant

Nettles **continued**

because I use Fenugreek tea. I always gather and dry a bit of nettles and place in 1 cup size tea bags. To use place one bag in 1 cup of boiling water. Let set steeping until cool. This acts on milk the same as a junket tablet. It can be used any place a junket tablet is needed like ice cream, cheese, yogurt and puddings. Our forefathers used nettles extensively for everything from food to a cure-all for most all ailments. When gathering nettle cover your arms and legs, and wear gloves. (See Bread Pudding recipe in Wild Violet section.)

Japanese Knotweed (Polygonum cuspidatum) grows wild, having escaped from cultivation after being imported from Japan as an ornamental. It's dried for Fall flower arrangements and it can also be used as a food. These recipes are for the young shoots leafing out. Do harvest the red bracket in the fall for winter bouquets. A plant of beauty and for food.

Japanese Knotweed
Polygonum cuspidatum

Japanese Knotweed Salad

To boiling salted water, drop in your knotweed shoots. Cover and turn off the heat to cool. Arrange on a serving plate and ladle over with salad dressing. Make this by mixing 1/2 cup salad dressing with 1/2 cup of cream. Garnish with a few violet blossoms. Looks so pretty and it is good too.

Japanese Knotweed Coffee Cake

2/3 cup bran cereal	1 1/2 cup sifted flour
2 teaspoons baking powder	1/2 teaspoon soda
1 cup knotweed stewed	1/2 cup milk
2 eggs	1/2 teaspoon salt
1/2 cup shortening	1 teaspoon orange extract.

Soak bran cereal in the milk. Add dry ingredients that have been sifted together. Add remaining ingredients and beat by hand 2 minutes. Finally, stir in 1 teaspoon orange extract. Bake at 350 degrees for 30 minutes in muffin tins or an 8-inch square pan. Sprinkle with confectionery sugar and serve with peach marmalade.

Japanese Knotweed Shoots Ham Loaf

1 cup cornflake crumbs
2 cups ground leftover ham
1/4 teaspoon cloves
1 cup stewed knotweed shoots
1 teaspoon molasses
2 eggs

Soften the crumbs with the knotweed and add the remaining ingredients. Mix and pack into loaf pan. Bake 350 degrees for about 1 hour. Serve with knotweed sauce.

Japanese Knotweed Sauce

1 cup stewed knotweed shoots
1 tablespoon butter.
1/2 cup raisins

Mix all together and simmer till the liquid has thickened. This sauce is good served with baked ham.

Japanese Knotweed Fish Butter

1 cup knotweed shoots
1/4 cup butter
Juice of 1 lemon

Slowly saute the knotweed in the butter till mushy. Mash with fork till it is a pulp. Remove from heat and stir in the lemon. Let cool and spread inside trout before cooking or serve as a sauce after fish is cooked. A nice butter, but a bit sour.

Milkweed (Asclepias syriaca) is a handsome plant growing about waist high. The young shoots can be cooked as a pot herb. In all stages, it exudes a milky glue like sap. Some experimentation was done in World War II on the milky sap as a substitute for glue. The fluffy fiber of the mature pod can be spun and was researched for fill in life preservers to replace Kapok. It took so much of this fiber and the milky glue that it was not deemed feasible. As a food, it is quite good after parboiling in about 3 waters.

Milkweed grows in open fields and roadways. It is one of the better known wild foods and can be eaten in all stages, if it is cooked. Never eat it raw, but then I don't think you would want to with all that milky glue like sap. Milkweed will start maturing about the end of the spring season. I rarely gather the milkweed till the poke crop is finished. The green leaf can be gathered up until the buds form.

Milkweed
Asclepias syriaca

I usually gather in the mid-morning and then cover with water till I'm ready to finish the job. I always give my weeds, of whatever kind, a salty water bath. I use 3 tablespoons of Kosher Pickling Salt to 1 gallon cold water. I fix the water, add the buds then sprinkle on the salt. Place a plate and weight down to keep the plant under the water so the bugs will come to the top. Your milkweed needs to be placed in water, and brought to a full rolling boil, then drained. You must do this 2 or 3 times with the milkweed pot herbs, pods and buds. My favorite way of using milkweed is the flower buds. After parboiling twice, plunge in cold water and freeze a quantity for Winter use. I don't care for broccoli but these flower pods can be used in any recipe in which you use cooked broccoli. A friend of mine cans hers like green beans.

Milkweed Buds and Butter Sauce

Use 4 cups flower buds cooked. Pour over sauce made of 1/2 cup melted butter with 1 tablespoon sugar, 1/4 cup flour and 1 teaspoon salt stirred in. Add 3/4 cup water and bring to a boil. Add zest with juice of 1 lemon. Remove from fire. Serve over toast.

Milkweed with Rice and Cheese

Have cooked:

- 4 cups milkweed flower buds
- 4 cups white rice - cooked
- 1 pkg. cheese from box of macaroni prepared according to directions
- 1 chopped onion

Place all this in a greased casserole. Sprinkle with 1 cup bread crumbs. Sprinkle with paprika. Bake 30 minutes at 350 degrees. So as not to waste anything, the macaroni will become a pasta salad.

Milkweed Soup

Use 5 cups milkweed flowerets parboiled twice, 1/4 cup butter to saute, 3/4 cup sliced scallions and 2 carrots diced. I have tried wild carrots but they are so tough and I would much rather enjoy the flowers. If I am getting the carrots from my garden I will chop up a few tops in the soup pot. Add 3 cups chicken broth and 1 tablespoon salt and cook till tender. Strain out the vegetables and puree in the blender. Return to the soup pot with the stock and 1 cup Half and Half and 1/2 cup fresh mint leaves. Heat but don't boil. Serve with crusty garlic bread.

Milkweed Pods

Gather and clean as for greens. The pods should be very small and immature about the length of the first joint of your thumb. Cut in half and parboil in salted water. Drain. Roll in cracker crumbs. Fry gently turning well in some of your ramp or garlic olive oil. I believe you will be pleasantly surprised.

Milkweed Flower Syrup

Let the flowers now come in to full bloom. They will smell so heavenly and can be used in cut flower arrangements. Mostly I dry some for my wreaths and potpourri. The bees will be busy gathering nectar from these plants. Always leave some of any of your plants for the wildlife of this planet. Some wild greens have bugs but never to the extent of our garden plants. If I find a plant that is buggy, I just go on my way and I will find a patch without bugs. Always remember if a bug can eat it, you can too. The size of the patch you find will determine how much you will have to gather and prepare. Wash and place to dry, then use for tea or syrup. Gather the blossoms and dry before making the tea.

Use 1 cup well packed dried blooming flowers. Cover with 2 cups boiling water and let sit to steep 30 minutes in a covered stainless steel pan. Drain. No need to parboil the blossoms. To each cup of the flower tea add 1 cup white sugar and 1/4 teaspoon cream of tartar. Boil this and reduce to 1/2. Bottle. A unique flavor all of its own for waffles or pancakes.

Milkweed Tea

Hot tea is made just with steeping the flower heads in water. I sweeten with honey.

Cold Milkweed Drink

I like this best. Just add some of your milkweed blossom syrup to a glass of soda or plain water and stir. Add ice cubes.

Sassafras (Sassafras albidum) grows abundantly here in the hills of West Virginia. If you know none or few of the usable herbs, chances are you have drank tea from the root of the sassafras tree. There is only one way to make this tea and it is different from the other wild teas or store-bought tea. First, you gather or dig the root of a large tree. Scrub this with a stiff brush and scrape off the outer layer. A wood rasp is the way I do it and brush again. Now you are at the part you want--the thick juicy layer next to the wood. Peel this off and put on a screen to dry. This all should be done the day you dig the root. The bark when dry and stored in a sealed jar and in a dark place will last several years.

You will not need a big piece because it is very potent. A piece about the size of your thumb nail will make several cups of hot tea. Now another question that comes up is about whether it is the red or yellow sassafras root you dig. Well, I've been digging sassafras for 50 years and they are really the same however, where the tree grows and the time of the year makes all of the difference in the world to how the root looks and how your tea tastes. The time to dig sassafras is after the ground has frozen and before the spring thaw. That is when the sap is full of all the goodness in the root bark. I also think that the older the tree, the richer and more full bodied the flavor will be. If you take out a good size root you will not damage the tree, but find another tree for the next year's

Sassafras
Sassafras albidum

roots, not this same one. This way you will not have ruined the whole tree. You can take any plant what you need but never destroy and always leave some for others. If you can find a construction site and get a whole root, so much the better. You'll have a supply for the whole family and this is the easiest for most folk.

If you dig the tiny roots, you will not be able to remove the inner bark; it's too thin. You will need to boil the whole root. It will take much more sassafras and your tea will have very little flavor. I guess I've made several hundred gallons of sassafras tea in my lifetime and the inner bark is best.

Believe me when I tell you no one from the Appalachian Mountains will ever believe sassafras tea will hurt you. A few years ago it was reported to cause cancer in mice and others may believe it, but we sure don't. I have also made jelly and hard tack candy from the tea. Here you need a real strong tea, and a bit of pulverized root bark to get the flavor. I have made gallons of this jelly, too, but not much of the Hard Tack, mostly because I'm not a candy eater.

Sassafras Tea

Place 4 cups cold water in a stainless steel, glass or granite pan with a dome lid. Put a piece of sassafras bark about the length of your thumb in with the water. Simmer, leaving lid in place, about one hour. The lid is important as the steam hits the lid it distills the oil from the sassafras and gives off the flavor. If too strong in flavor, add more water. You may be able to make tea over the piece of sassafras again.

Sassafras Jelly

1/2 cup strong sassafras tea — 1 1/2 cups apple juice
1 teaspoon powdered sassafras — 1 box Sure-Jel

Heat and stir together. Bring to full rolling boil, one you can't stir down. Have ready 5 cups of white sugar, add all at once. Bring to a boil again, stirring all the time. Boil 1 minute and pour into sterilized jars. Seal by placing in a hot water bath for 10 minutes. These make super gifts or bazaar items.

Sassafras Jelly from Honey

3 cup honey — 1 box pectin
2 cups strong sassafras tea
2 tablespoons powdered sassafras bark

Add one box pectin to the hot tea, stirring continually to a full rolling boil. Add 3 cups of honey and boil again. When it reaches a full boil, cook 1 minute, stirring and counting 100 and 100-1, 100-2 till you reach 160. Then remove from heat and seal.

Sassafras Candy

3 3/4 cups white sugar — 1 cup strong sassafras tea
1-3 tablespoons powdered bark — 1 1/2 cups white corn syrup

Combine in a heavy sauce pan, stirring with a wooden spoon all the time. Boil until temperature reaches 310 degrees on candy thermometer or to hard crack stage. Pour in a buttered 7-ince square pan. While still warm, mark into small squares. As soon as it is cool enough, break apart and dust with confectionery sugar.

Sassafras leaves--I have been experimenting with the leaves since I read it is very popular stuff in Cajun Country. It seems strange to me. As far as I know, no West Virginian ever used the dry powdered leaves for anything except nibbling. Usually I eat a few leaves on a long hike. I sometimes put the tender tops of a young plant in my salad bowl. But

Sassafras continued

to check out these dried leaves, I set off one day to gather me some leaves. After drying, I had a nice green powder with not much taste. So lest you think writing a book is all fun and games, come on to the kitchen. Start with the water and that won't harm the true taste. I used 1 cup water with 1 tablespoon or more of file', what is commonly called the leaf of the sassafras tree. After boiling, all I have is green slime.

Well, let's put it into the refrigerator to see what happens. Next day, I still have green slime. Well, let's try it again--heat and add 1 tablespoon of dried powdered leaf of sassafras. Next boil and stir a bit, it now smells good in any case. Into the refrigerator again. Next day, well now I have a thick green slime something akin to digest of a cow.

I read it is used much in Louisiana cooking and is added after the cooking is complete. For now, I'll leave it alone and maybe someday I will go to Louisiana and learn how to use dried grown sassafras leaves or as they call it file'.

Sassafras green leaves make a good substitute for thyme in whatever recipe.

Root Beer

Use 1/2 pound bark cut into strips. This can be all birch bark or half birch bark and a bit of ginger and spicebush bark. Cover these with water and simmer. While still warm, strain out the bark and stir in sugar or honey (about 4 cups or to your taste). Pour this into a five gallon container and fill with water. Dissolve a package of yeast and stir in. Cover and keep in a cool place until it ferments. Strain and jug, then store in refrigerator so it will ferment no more. Enjoy. Really, this has never lasted long enough to cap and bottle it. To many of my folks' bottles exploded so now with refrigeration and the products on hand all the time, it can be made more often. If you must bottle and cap, these and other beer making supplies can be ordered from Nichols Garden Nursery, 1190 North Pacific Highway, Albany, Oregon 97321.

Versatile Poke

Poke (Phytolacca americana), or poke weed, grows around disturbed land and is rather hard to eradicate after it gets established. One large clump can be maintained in the corner of your garden, and will be all the average family will use. It can be forced in the winter by waiting until after freezing weather, digging and placing it in a tub of moist sand. The sprouts will keep returning as they are harvested, however, don't plan to reharvest it again in the spring.

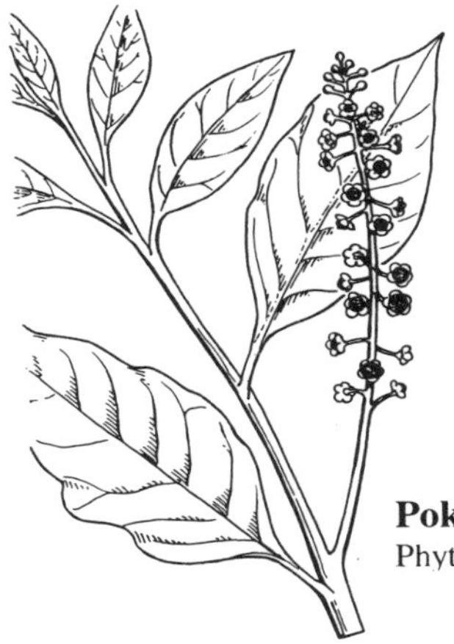

Pokeweed
Phytolacca americana

By maintaining two plant clumps, one for the winter and one for the spring, you can eat pretty much year-round, and, yes, I like it that much. The roots are poison as well as the mature stalk, mature leaves and berries, so you will only gather the poke in the spring until the stalks get tough and it starts to bloom. However, the berries are used by many as a cure for arthritis or rheumatism and you can't convince them that the berries are harmful. I have tried them with no ill effect and believe that you would have to eat a very large quantity to cause a problem. I doubt anyone would want to eat many as the taste is awful.

In using poke greens you must parboil at least once for young leaves and twice for the older ones. However, when using the stalk all one needs to do is peel off the outer layer and the bitter is gone.
In the early spring, the first poke to appear will have a long, pink, soft stalk with only a few tiny leaves. After harvesting, I wash and parboil, cook briefly and serve with a bit of butter, salt and pepper.

By the time of the next picking, the plant will be about a foot high and the stalk will be some greener and leaves formed. Gather, wash, chop both stalks and leaves then parboil, usually once will do. Fry in bacon and ham grease with a bit of salt and pepper. Indeed, ham and cornbread are nice accompaniments for your greens.

After frying the ham and removing from the skillet, drain off the fat and add the poke. Heat. All of the pot liquid will be in your greens as seasoning.

When I was growing up, a couple of good messes of poke greens were just a natural thing, but now I use them year-round in many ways. I have them in the freezer for winter use too. The poke continues to grow to three to five feet, and the stalk is larger. When the poke is about an inch in diameter, I harvest the stalks. They must be peeled for pickles and creamed poke stalk. You do not need to parboil peeled stalks. If you use the leaves, they will probably need to be parboiled twice. Poke has a very distinctive taste and lots of things come into play with its growing and taste. A plant growing in hard clay and full sun will be much stronger in taste than one growing by a barn and only partially in the sun. The amount of rain makes a difference, and, in a dry year, I will not be able to harvest as many times. Then, when it sets blossom buds, the poke season is over for another year.

Poke Pickles

Gather and peel the stalks. Make a pickle solution of 1 cup vinegar, 1 cup white sugar, heat and stir to dissolve the sugar. Now, add about 4 cups of peeled and sliced poke stalk. Heat to boiling and pack in a sterile quart jar. Let sit for about a week and I betcha' you can't eat just one!

In working up this recipe, I have added wild mustard or hot pepper seeds, but after much sampling, I like it best with just the vinegar-sugar solution. You might like to try a seasoning of your choice.

Creamed Polk Stalks

Prepare the stalks and cook in salt water with a lot of butter. Prepare a hard sauce with milk and corn starch and add, stirring until thickened. Serve with toast or cornbread.

Poke Pennies

Gather, peel and slice 4 cups of the poke stalk. Cook in salt water 10 minutes, drain. Beat 1 egg with 1 tablespoon milk. Dip the poke penny in 1/2 cup cracker crums and 1/2 cup cornmeal, then the egg wash and, again, in the crumb mix. Saute 1 whole green onion in a bit of oil. Remove. Fry your pople pennnies till brown on both sides.

Poke Omelette

Crumble 1/2 pound sausage in an electric skillet. Sit temperature 340 degrees, fry and drain off the fat. Add 4 cups of cooked poke leaves that have been chopped. Beat 6 eggs with 1/2 cup milk and pour over the sausage and poke. Add 1 cup shredded cheese and about 1/2 cup chopped young onions. Proceed as you would for an omelette and serve with cornbread muffins.

If you are feeding poke to someone for the first time, this is a good way to do it with the omelette. Grandma always said waste not want not. Don't discard the stems. I always have more stems then leaves, expecially when freezing, as I never freeze stalks. They can be used as extenders to creamed peas, onions, corns, carrots and most soups. They don't distract from the flavor and look at all those good things you are adding--things like calcium, phosphorus, iron, vitamin A and C plus lots of fiber--and all for free!

Dandelions

O lordy, "dandelions (Taraxacum officinale) all over and cursed by many." If you will use the dandelion instead of battling it, life could be easier. Several uses can be found for this plant, such as vegetable oysters, coffee-like brew, pot herbs, or most any place greens are needed. It is supposed to clear the liver. Be sure that when you gather this, there is no pesticide, herbicide or fertilizers on the lawn.

Dandelions
Taraxacum officinale

To brew--gather, wash and dry the roots. Then roast till they are dark, at least dark as coffee. Grind. I always mix my roots with coffee. No one ever knows the difference, unless you tell them. Chicory can be used in the same way.

Vegetable Oyster

1 quart of opened flower buds washed and dried
1 egg beaten well

Dip the buds and roll in 1 cup flour that has been mixed with 1 table-spoon salt and pepper. Fry in butter slowly, browning on both sides. An electric skillet set at 340 degrees is what I use. I betcha' can't eat just one.

Dandelion Leaf Salad

Gather and clean the leaves you will need for the size of your family. These must be gathered early in the spring before blooming. Fry a few strips of bacon till crisp, remove and crumble. Drain off most of the fat and using same skillet, add 1/2 cup vinegar and 1/2 cup of sugar till boiling. Pour over the chopped leaves and mix well until they are all wilted. Add a few green young onions and stir again. Last, add the bacon pieces to the top. Serve and enjoy. I usually have this with cornbread and beans.

If you don't want that fat, just add a little margarine and cook greens till the water has evaporated and garnish with a sliced boiled egg.

Leftover cooked greens work well in cheese omelets or quiche.

Dandelion Wine

Into a large wooden wine barrel, add

1 bushel clean dandelion blossoms and buds.
25 pounds of raisins
10 pounds wheat berry enclosed in a clean muslin bag
35 gallons of spring or rain water
50 pounds of sugar dissolved in water
2 dozen chopped oranges or peaches or equal amount of grapes

Stir each day with a wooden paddle that has only been used for this purpose. Never have any metal around your wine When it stops bubbling, strain off the solids. Let sit in barrel to age. Sample. Strain off. Bottle. I have never made this wine. It is said to be very good. The recipe has been handed down over 100 years in my family.

Purslane (Portulaca oleracea) is one wild food I had never eaten. I knew you could and also I know folks who love it. After battling that garden weed all my younger years and hating it, how could I eat it? So for this book I had to give it a try. It is a very drought-resistant hardy plant plus being pretty. You could dig it out and it would just lay there till it rained and then start growing all over again. I would have to dig it again. Many times when hoeing the garden, we would rake it up and feed it to the pigs or chickens. At least, that way it stayed put and I didn't have to dig it again. But if it had bloomed, look out for those seeds and next year's crop. The leaves and stem are mucilaginous. After washing and chopping, pour over some boiling water to get rid of that.

The young tender tips are fine in salads as is, and I use them in stirfry. It's strange after working with this plant, I found lots of ways to use and like it. Somewhere in my earlier years I developed a prejudice to purslane. Many folks have this same prejudice about plants as well as wild meats and don't even know why. This is a shame and maybe they just don't know what they are missing. Really that's what this work of mine is all about: preserving these old ways and making some memories.

Purslane
Portulaca oleracea

I made an especially good dish from this plant. At today's standards, it's quite time-consuming, but my foremothers labored long and lovingly over nutritious foods placed in front of their family. I have learned to use it now quite extensively. When found growing, it goes in all my pot herbs, soups, salad bowls and then into other things. When cooking it alone, I parboil first and then season with salt, pepper and a few ham or bacon pieces. Return to heat and simmer to evaporate the liquid. Serve this as a side dish. When it is leftover, purslane is good in quiche, omelets and I sometimes put it in croquettes.

The way I like it best is stuffed mashed potatoes. Using your leftover mashed potatoes, a bit of meat and your purslane or other greens, you can make a whole new meal.

Stuffed Potatoes with Purslane

Take 2 cups of day-old leftover mashed potatoes, add 1 beaten egg, 1 cup white flour, mix well. Divide your potatoes into equal parts. Roll on a floured board to resemble a potato. Make a hole down the center and fill with filling. Make the filling by grinding a bit of meat, purslane and the tops of one wild onion and a sprinkle of Parmesan cheese mixed all together. Push the potato dough up and over the filling covering all. Roll in flour and fry, turning to brown on all sides.

Pickled Purslane Stems

After gathering the purslane when it is mature, remove the tips and leaves for pot herbs. The stems are pink and can be rather large. Chop in 1-2 inch pieces. Heat pieces to boiling at the same time you also heat 1 cup vinegar mixed with 1 cup sugar. Place pieces in a jar and pour the vinegar over. Seal. You may want to add a slice of onion, pickling spices or horseradish for more flavor.

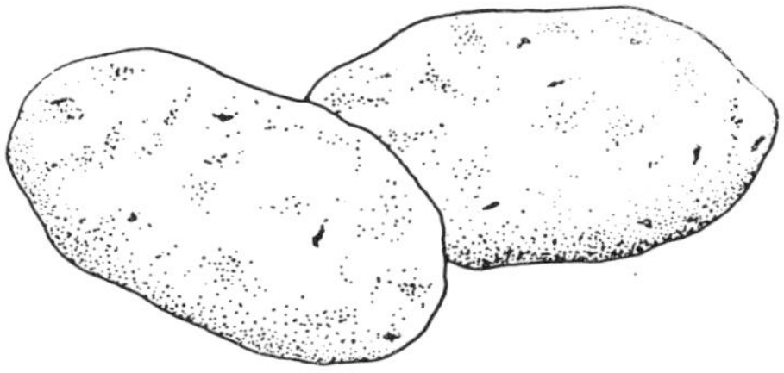

Jerusalem Artichoke, or sun choke (Helianthus tuberosus), as it is sometimes called, is nothing at all like the globe artichoke. It grows four to five feet tall with a yellow flower head, resembling a small sunflower. The part used is the knobby root that resembles a potato. It is a native American plant and was transported back to the old world by some of the first settlers. Indians taught the settlers of its use. It grows wild over most of the United States. Some work has been done on breeding of these roots till now we have long skinny roots as well as the plump knobby ones. Some are red and yellow somewhat like potatoes. The similarity ends in the appearance, as they in no way taste like potato. Here in West Virginia, you must protect a patch to keep deer from completely destroying it. Once you decide to have the Jerusalem artichokes, plant them where they are to stay and dig up all you can find each winter or they may soon take over. I cut the stalks off and mulch in the fall and dig all winter as needed. They need to be used when dug as they shrink up when exposed to air. If wanting to store them, I just cover with water. They're hard to clean. The way I do it is that first, I spray them with a high pressure water hose, then I scrub them with a brush. I rarely peel, but just use skin and all.

Jerusalem Artichoke
Helianthus tuberosus

The artichokes can be used in many ways, but I prefer them raw or pickled. They have a nice crunchy feel, like the water chestnut, and a nutty flavor. I have gathered them from the wild, and they sometimes taste earthy from the soil. These I pass by, and look for others that are better. Long ago, I established my plot below my chicken house. It has prospered well. I would miss them terribly if they were gone. I add them to roasts, stirfry them and have made everything from soup to dessert from them.

Raw Jerusalem Artichokes

To keep them from discoloring, slice raw chokes and place them in a vinegar bath of 1 tablespoon vinegar to 1 cup water.

Jerusalem Artichoke Kraut

Grate your chokes and place in the bottom of your pickling jar up about 3/4 full. Now add small chokes both sliced and whole. This is to keep the small grated pieces from floating to the top. Dissolve 1/2 cup pickling salt and add to the jar. Continue as you do for pickles. If some of these grated pieces float to the top, they will turn brown and probably spoil. This kraut is very good raw. I sometimes use it in rye bread.

Kraut Rye Bread

3/4 cup boiling water	1 tablespoon honey or molasses
1 tablespoon salt	1 tablespoon butter
2 packages dry yeast	1/4 cup warm water
4 cups coarsely ground rye flour	1 cup choke-kraut

Chop and drain the kraut. Combine boiling water, molasses or honey, salt and butter in a warmed bowl. Stir till the butter melts. Sprinkle the yeast over the warm water in a cup to dissolve, then stir into the butter mixture when cool enough. Add 2 cups of the flour and beat well. Add the kraut. Mix in remaining flour, mixing in with hands. Turn dough out to a floured board and kneed hard for 10 minutes. This is important and don't cut the time short. Also, you will have a better loaf if you use half wheat flour, but since I'm allergic to wheat, I use all rye. Turn dough into a greased bowl. Cover and let rise till double in bulk. Punch down and kneed again. Set to rise and when double in size, divide into two pieces. Shape in loaves. Let rise and brush top with milk. Let rise again till double in size. Bake 400 degrees for about 30 minutes or until it sounds hollow when thumped.

Jerusalem Artichoke Salad

Boil a few chokes in salt water till tender (about half the time it takes to boil potatos). Peeling is optional. Slice and combine with sliced scallions and a bit of salad greens. I usually have cress growing and use one of these. Mix with cooked/boiled salad dressing (see below) salt and pepper, toss. Arrange on lettuce and garnish with boiled eggs.

Boiled Salad Dressing

1 egg	1/4 cup flour
1 cup sugar	2 tablespoons butter
1 cup vinegar	1 teaspoon salt
1 cup milk	1 teaspoon dry mustard

Beat egg, add sugar, salt, flour, mustard and milk. Add vinegar. Place in a double boiler and cook until thick. Add the butter and stir to melt.

Pickled Jerusalem Artichokes

Pickle chokes in a one gallon sterilized jar with layers of artichoke, carrot, onion and cauliflower. To 1 cup of hot water, dissolve 1/4 cup of pickling salt. Pour over the vegetables and add water to fill the jar. Now, find a glass or jelly jar that will fit in the top of the gallon jar. Fill this with water and set in place to keep the vegetables from being exposed to the air. I then let them set on or in my kitchen sink. The solution will start fermenting, and the bubbling brine will come out of the jar. When bubbling stops, they are ready to eat. Refrigerate or keep in a cool place. Always keep the pickles covered and never exposed to the air. The chokes can be done alone but the addition of vegetables gives a better flavor. I have tried most vegetables with them and turnips work especially well.

Eating the Wild Rose

The wild rose of several species grows in open woods and pastries from Maine to Texas and West to the Rockies. The flower petals can be made into several things and the hips are made into jelly, syrups and teas. Unfortunately, I rarely find enough to make much of anything. The deer, turkey and other wildlife always seem to get there before me. Not to be outdone, however, I dug several and placed them in my flower garden.

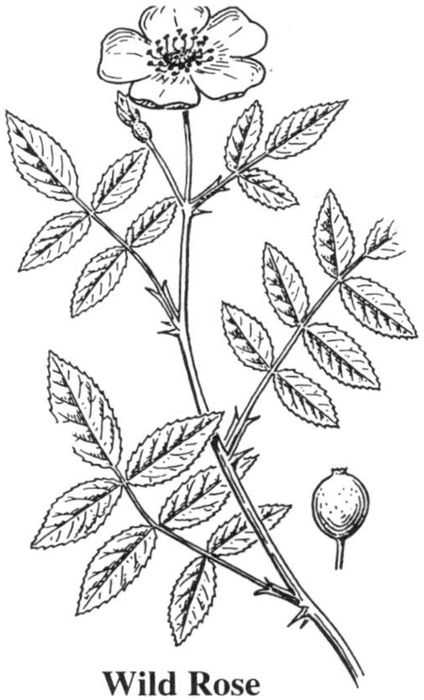

Wild Rose
Rosa carolina

I gave them a try and was pleasantly surprised. Thereafter, my use of wild roses for potpourri has declined considerably over the years.

I let the rose come to full bloom and just before it is to shatter and fall, I grasp the full flower head in my hand and pull. Usually I have a handful of petals to work with, but it is still never enough. The more aroma the rose has, the better the end product. Never use roses that have been sprayed. If you can find the wild roses, they are better, but if not, try with the older varieties of roses. Sometimes, the lower part of the petal where it joins the stem is bitter; mine is not, so I use the complete petal. I have no idea the name of this rose.

Wild Rose Petal Vinegar

1 cup well-packed dried, fresh or frozen petals covered with 2 cups boiling white vinegar. Cover this to steep. Remove from the heat. Stir down the rose petals before the vinegar cools completely. Let this sit over night. Use only glass or stainless utensils when making. Strain through a coffee filter into a glass jar. Seal and store in a cool dark cupboard.

Wild Rose Petal Salad Dressing

Mix 2 cups white sugar with 1 cup water. Stir and heat to boiling. Cool completely and add to the rose vinegar. Mix with the best olive oil you can find to make an excellent dressing. Use this on mild flavored salad ingredients, leaving out the garlic and adding very little onion since they will overpower the delicate rose flavor.

Wild Rose Water

1 cup well-packed fresh rose petals. Pour over 1 cup boiling rain water. Cover and let this sit overnight. Strain and refrigerate. Mist this on your face and pamper your complexion. Use this up quickly as it has no preservative to keep over a long period of time.

Wild Rose Honey

4 cups well-packed rose petals	2 cups boiling water
2 lbs clear flavored honey	4 tablespoons butter

Gather an prepare the petals and place in a quart glass jar. Add the boiling water, stir, cover and let partially cool. Shake so all petals are covered. Let set until the next day (24 hours). Strain. Warm the honey and butter so it is syrupy, now stir in the rose water. Place in a covered glass jar and refrigerate until using. Use this on toast, muffins, pancakes, cereal or ice cream. I like this better made from the dried rose petals and buds. This is usually made later in the year when I have the clear honey and am not so busy.

Rose Petal Jam

Pour 3 cups boiling water over a quart of fresh rose petals. Let sit covered to steep. Drain off the water and make sure you have a full cup of wilted rose petals. Strain the water and add enough to have the original needed 3 cups. Add 1 box powdered pectin, 3 tablespoons rose vinegar and 1 tablespoon oil. Stir and bring to a boil. Add 4 cups sugar all at once and continue to stir till it comes to a full rolling boil. Add the rose petals. Boil 1 minute more and pour into sterilized jars. This will keep in the refrigerator for 2 months. If you want it to keep longer, place in canning jars with lids and process in a hot water bath for 5 minutes.

Rose Hip Tea

In a pan with a lid, steep 3-4 rose hips in 1 cup of hot water for 30 minutes. Strain and serve with honey.

Freezer Rose Hip Jam

The best recipe I have found for this is Euell Gibbon's--see page 169 of his book, <u>Stalking the Healthful Herbs</u>.

Wild Violets (Viola Spp.) are those pretty little purple flowers that come up all over in the spring. They are chocked full of nice vitamins, especially vitamin C. As a child, I don't remember using them for anything, but the leaves in pot herbs or eating raw. The flowers were picked for bouquets, potpourri and for pressed pictures. Grandma always said "beware if you found violets blooming on your land in the fall. There would be a death in the family by spring." Sometimes, I believe my forebearers did really believe such sayings. If you are going to make much of violets, be prepared for a long day of picking or do as I do. As I am gathering my greens and pot greens, I keep a small container just for violet blossoms. I pick, then place in the refrigerator until I have enough for whatever recipe I am making. I especially like the violet syrup drink and the green leaves both cooked and in salad. I have kept the blossom in the refrigerator crisper for a week before using. I have canned the flowers by packing them in the jar and covering with hot water. I then place the jar in the canner of hot water and boil for 15 minutes. They don't seem as good, but it can be done; however, should be used in a few months. I have also frozen them for later use. I prefer to enjoy them in season, then move on to something else.

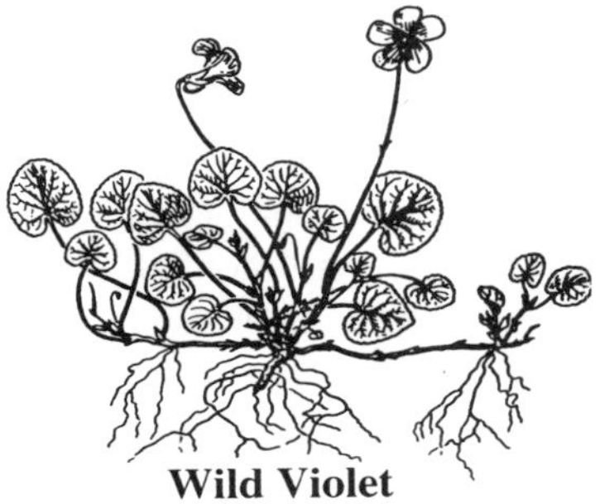

Wild Violet
Viola appalachiensis

Wild Violet Syrup

Violet syrup is made by picking one quart of the violet flowers and covering with boiling water. Let this sit as is for 24 hours. Strain, add juice of one lemon and 1 1/2 cups white sugar. Stir and bring to boil. Place in a sterilized jar, cap and refrigerate.

For a drink--pour glass about 1/4 full, add ice and water. Enjoy.

Wild violets continued

Boiled Pudding Ball

The syrup can be used for pancakes, ice cream and especially on the old bread pudding my Grandma made and here's how. Take one half loaf of stale homebaked bread and trim off the crust. Crumble this in 1 pint of milk, 2 tablespoons butter, 1/2 cup sugar or honey. Beat 3 egg yolks and add them. Now beat the egg whites and fold them in. You can use this puddling with various sauces so add whatever spice you desire. Have on the stove a large 4 quart pan with lid, rack and 2 quarts of water boiling. Take a plastic roaster bag (large size) and cut in half. Lay this over a 2 quart mixing bowl. Pour in the bread batter and gather up all the sides. Tie the top closed near the top to leave room for the batter to expand and keep the bag from bursting. Place this ball of plastic-covered pudding into the boiling water. Cover and cook, boiling slowly, for two hours. Don't remove the lid until finished. Remove from heat and let sit until serving time. It can be served hot or cold. Hot it is served with the meat and a vegetable course, covered with gravy. For dessert, it is best cold with whipped cream, fruits or syrups. This recipe came from my Great Grandmother and can be prepared, as she did, in a kettle over an open fire when no stove or oven is available. My Grandmother used muslin to wrap hers in and it was often hung on a rafter for eating any time.

Wild Violet Jelly

2 cups violet flowers (no stems), 2 1/2 cups boiled water poured over. Let sit and steep. Drain. To 2 cups of this infusion, add the juice of one lemon. Add 1 box Sure-Jel. Place on high heat and bring to boil. Add 4 cups of sugar all at once and stir until a full boil returns. Boil for 1 full minute. Skim, jar and seal.

Sugared Wild Violet Flowers

Wash, pat dry with towel, dip in beaten egg whites and powder with confectionery sugar, covering both sides. Place blossoms on a plate that has been sprinkled with sugar. Turn and re-sugar several times a day until dry. After they are dry, store in a covered dark jar. These can be used to decorate a special cake or eaten as candy.

Wild Violet Tea

Any leaves you don't use in pot herbs can be dried for tea. Small cup size tea bags can be purchased for your teas, but mostly I make pot size tea bags by placing a handful of dried leaves in the center of a coffee filter and tie at the top. Do try violets just once and you will be delightfully surprised.

Lamb's Quarter (Chenopedium spp.), also known as wild spinach or pigsweed, is abundant and grows in disturbed ground. I encourage it to grow in my garden, always leaving one that will grow about 6 feet tall. By clipping and using its tip ends, I encourage it to branch. The grown plant gives me seeds. They are stripped off the plant and put to dry. Rubbing them over a fine sieve gives me all the seeds I want. What is left can be used in stews, topping for casseroles or in breads to all fiber and nutrients. The seeds I use similar to poppy seeds. As the others come up in the garden, I harvest. I like them better than spinach and they grow all summer. I use this plant most any place I need spinach. As the plant grows older and blooms, I will strip off the seed head and small leaves and use them in the place of broccoli in soup and the broccoli-cheese casserole. These are very much like raab (the Italian broccoli, I like very much).

Lamb's Quarter
Chenopedium album

Lamb's Quarter Casserole

1 gallon fresh greens	Sprinkle of paprika
1 small jar of Cheez Whiz	4 tablespoons butter
1/4 cup milk	2 cups cooked rice
1 cup dried bread crumbs with	
1 tablespoon butter to help hold them together	

Cook greens. Mix the cheese, milk and rice. Fold in the greens. Place in a greased casserole dish. Sprinkle with 1 cup dry bread crumbs. Dot with butter and sprinkle with paprika. Bake 350 degrees 30 minutes or until browned and bubbly. Any leftover meat may be chopped and added.

Lamb's quarter continued

Lamb's Quarter Soup

3 cups cooked Lamb's Quarter
2 tablespoons butter
Dash of hot sauce
1/2 cup water
1/4 teaspoon oriental five-spice
1/2 cup wild onion tops
4 cups chicken stock
Salt and pepper to taste
4 tablespoons cornstarch
1 can evaporated milk

Place the cooked lambs quarter in soup pot. Saute the chopped wild onion tops in the butter. Mix enough of the chicken stock to cook. Add the spices. Cook all together until the onion tops are tender. Pour into a blender and puree. Pour back onto the soup pot and add the remainder of the chicken broth. Bring to a boil. Mix cornstarch with water and stir in. Cook until thickened. Remove from heat and stir in the canned milk and adjust seasoning. Serve garnished with fresh wild onion tops. If you like this a little thicker, add a few sprinkles of instant mashed potatoes. I usually blanch and freeze lambs quarter for winter use. If I have any left by ramp season, I use the ramps (4 whole) instead of the wild onions.

Stewed Lamb's Quarter and Pudding

Chicken parts--backs, wings and / or necks
4 cups cooked lamb's quarter
Salt / pepper
1 batter pudding (found in Wild Violet section)

Cook the chicken parts in water, enough to cover, the day before preparing the dish. Skim off the fat, pick off meat and discard bones. Add salt and pepper to the broth and add enough green lambs quarter to equal 4 cups cooked. When tender, add the pudding bag and continue cooking following these directions. A whole stewing chicken can be used, but I prefer it this way. See Violet chapter for pudding bag recipe.

Wild Fruits and Berries

Wild Apple

The wild apples I refer to here are seedlings from some of the old variety of apples that are almost all now gone. They were accidentally planted both by humans and animals. They have their own flavor and size. They're never very pretty, but they do produce. In a bad apple year, all those nice fancy dwarf apple trees will not produce. Go walking and find a wild one with plenty of fruit. They grow naturally with no spray, pruning or care. Their flavor will be one you will never forget. It seems a shame the old flavorful apples have been lost to the next generations. A few hardy folks are preserving some of these trees. If there was ever a better apple than the Summer Queen, I have never tasted it, but I can find no seedlings. Indeed, both the Starks Delicious and Granny Smith were found growing wild and then bred to the apple we know today. Some trees will be better than others and if a seed from a dwarf tree is planted, it's fruit will not be good. If an apple tree can produce in the wild this way, are we humans any better off: What with all our hybridized, sprayed, dwarfed, processed, sterilized, polished, picked green and packed food in our bodies, how much better off are we? Would we be better off living more like the wild foods that nature prepares. However, that is a whole other ball game, and I guess I'll do as I please. Everyone is to his or her own opinion and I've expressed mine. You do likewise. These apples can be used anywhere apples are called for.

Wild Apple
Pyrus malus

The Boiled Apple Dumplings recipe is a very old one and it is much requested, so I have included it here. The older generation remembers them well and you might just like them, too.

Boiled Apple Dumplings

2 cups flour	1/3 cup shortening
1 tablespoon sugar	1 teaspoon salt
3 teaspoons baking powder	2/3 cup milk

Stir the dry ingredients, cut in the shortening and mix in the milk. Let the dough rest while you prepare the apples and get the kettle boiling. Peel and core 4 apples. Fill the center with a teaspoon of butter, filling the remainder of the hole with sugar and sprinkle with cinnamon. Cut the dough into 4 pieces. Roll and place the apple in the center. Moisten the edges of the dough all the way around. Bring the dough up over the apple and pinch to seal. Pierce the dough around the apple with a fork. Pick up in your hand and squeeze gently to expel the air. Place in the pot of boiling water that has a rack or upside down plate in the bottom. Cover and gently boil for 30 minutes. Don't remove lid till done. Lift out the dumplings with a slotted spoon and serve with cream or milk dip. If you want baked apple dumplings, place each dough-wrapped apple in a well-oiled muffin pan. If you work your dough long enough and get it sealed completely, the dumpling will stay intact. If not, it will burst. Some folks wrapped these in cheesecloth to keep them intact but I cut up a plastic baking bag. Then, I place them to boil and they stay intact. Sometimes, I fix chunky applesauce in a pan and add two cups of water and place it in my apple dumplings. If they come apart, they are not so pretty, but still eat well. I use the chunky applesauce to pour over them.

West Virginia Apple Pie

Beat 1 egg. Add 3/4 cup sugar and continue beating. Add 1 teaspoon vanilla. Mix 1/3 cup self-rising flour to the egg mixture. Fold in 1 1/2 cups sliced raw apples and 1/2 cup nut meat of your choice. Pour into a well-oiled pie pan. Sprinkle with nutmeg. Bake in 350 degree preheated oven for 25 minutes. Serve warm. Seconds will be needed, so make two!!

If you want, you can substitute fresh peaches, but use almond flavoring instead of vanilla and mace instead of nutmeg.

Sauted Apple Slices

Peel and slice 4 cups of apples. Place in a buttered skillet and sprinkle with sugar. The sugar needed will depend on how sour the apples are, so start with 1/2 cup and add more, if needed. Fry slowly and stir often. Honey can be added if not sweet enough or instead of sugar. Cinnamon can be added also. These slices should remain whole and not be cooked to a mush. Serve hot with a meat dish.

Chunky Apple Sauce

In a sauce pan, put 1 cup water and 1 cup sugar. Stir and heat till sugar is dissolved. Add 4 cups of sliced raw apples. Cover and boil about 10 minutes. The apples should be mushy and chunky. This is usually served cold.

Apple Butter

Apple butter is really only apples, sugar and seasoning cooked slowly for a very long time. There are many variations, however. This recipe can be made in the oven or in a crock pot. Place 16 cups of peeled and sliced apples with 1 cup cider or cider vinegar in your crock pot and set on high. Cook for about 4 hours stirring from the bottom up so all apples will cook to a mush. Now, add sugar, one cup at a time, stirring after each addition. Cook 1 hour between each cup of sugar till you have it as sweet as you like. Continue cooking till a wooden spoon placed vertical in center of the container does not lean or sink. This means you've cooked the apple butter enough. Now it is time to add either oil of cinnamon or oil of clove and mix in well. I usually toss in 1/2 cup of cinnamon red hot candies. If you have only yellow apples, the cinnamon red hots will also give it color. Apples can also be washed, cored, cooked with the peeling on, and then pressed through colander, especially if they have pretty red skins and you choose to use only the oil. Do not try to make apple butter with sweet apples, as they will not cook up soft. Use your sweet apples for spiced apples, in salads or in any cooked dessert where a firm apple is required.

Apple Butter Cake

1 cup white sugar
1/2 cup margarine
4 eggs beaten
2 cups flour
1 teaspoon soda
1 teaspoon cinnamon
1/2 teaspoon clove
1/2 teaspoon nutmeg
1 cup apple butter
1/2 cup sour milk
2 teaspoons baking powder

Cream the butter and sugar, add eggs and beat well. Add apple butter and sour milk. Sift dry ingredients together and stir into the first mixture. Pour into 2 well-oiled and floured 9-inch cake pans. Bake in preheated 350 degree oven for 30 minutes. Cool and frost.

Bean-Apple Cake

2 cups leftover cooked dry beans mashed
1 cup sugar
2 egg whites slightly beaten
1 teaspoon baking soda
2 cups sliced raw apples
1/4 cup flavored Crisco
1 cup oat bran flour
1/2 cup chopped nuts
1 tablespoon spicewood berries ground
2 teaspoons maplene flavoring
1 cup finely chopped dried fruit

Cream the sugar and shortening. Add the egg whites and the mashed beans. Stir the dry ingredients together and stir into the first mixture. Fold in the apples, flavoring, nuts and dried berries. Pour in a well-oiled tube pan and bake at 350 degrees for about 1 hour. Turn out on rack and cool. Frost with a cream cheese frosting.

Dried Apple Slices

Peel and slice what amount of apples you have. Place slices in vinegar water solution for 30 minutes. Drain and place on screen to dry, and they will stay nearly white. For the vinegar-water solution, use 1 cup white vinegar for a gallon of cold water.

Wild Peaches

They are very prevalent here in West Virginia and can be encouraged to grow or pulled when they are young. Anytime anyone throws out a peach seed, unless a critter gets it, up will come a tree. They come up and produce in all sizes from the size of a hickory nut up to plum size but never get the size of the original. They can be freestone or cling, yellow-reddish or white. The flavors can be dull all the way up to the best peach you ever tasted. I encourage these seeds to grow and after the first fruiting (3-4 years), if the fruit is good, I keep the tree; if it's not so good, I will cull the tree out.

Wild Peach
Prunus persica

Grandma peeled every peach, quite a time consuming job, but mother didn't and I usually don't either. The peeling is roughage that we pay a big price for when we buy bran. It does not look so pretty but it's still good. You can use them any way you would other peaches: jam, jelly, butter, pies, jello, etc. If you have culled your trees, you will still have a better tasting dish then with purchased peaches. Some of these tree-ripened peaches are amazingly delicious--beyond description. Most folks in this younger generation have never seen a white peach let alone tasted one. The flavor is completely different from the usual yellow ones. As I write this today, I am preserving peaches in cold pack, dry, butter, brandy, pickled, marmalade and freezing. Some of my recipes follow and I'm sorry if you have no access to a wild peach tree to really taste the difference. Yes, I know that they are hard to find and peel. If peeling is needed, it will help if you pour boiling water over them, then plunge them into cold water.

Peach Pudding

Butter a round pyrex dish and fill half full with sliced peaches. In another bowl, mix 1/2 cup brown sugar with 2 tablespoons butter. Add 1 beaten egg. Add 1 cup self-rising flour alternately with 1/2 cup of either half and half, whole or goats milk. Add 1 teaspoon almond or vanilla extract. Beat well and pour over the peaches. Bake 350 degrees for about 30 minutes. Serve warm.

Peach Leathers

Wash and seed peaches. Cook till tender and mash through a foley mill or by another process of your choice. Spread on dry cookie sheets that have been greased. Then cut in strips and dust with confectionery sugar and store. This is eaten as is or cut into small pieces and put in granola.

Crock Peach Brandy

I prefer the white cling peach here, but I sometimes use yellow or mix them. The idea of all the foraging is using what you'll find. Prepare the peaches and layer in a crock with a layer of sugar and a layer of peaches. End with a layer of sugar, then each day add sugar till the juice is drawn and sugar dissolved. Weigh down with a plate and cover with several layers of muslin. Make sure all the peaches are below the surface or they will spoil. Let this sit till about Thanksgiving. Lift out the peaches and strain the liquid into bottles and store. These peaches are marvelous in mincemeat, and the brandy is marvelous for fruit cakes. If you are in a hurry, add a bottle of purchased peach brandy. You can then use it in about a week.

Brandied Peach Sauce

Take seeds from brandied peach to equal 1 cup. Saute in 2 tablespoons of butter. Add 1 cup water and heat. Thicken with 2 tablespoons corn starch. Serve hot or cold.

Peach Custard Pie

Prepare a 9" pie shell unbaked. Fill half full with sliced peaches. Beat 2 eggs and add 1/2 cup sugar, then 1/2 cup half and half milk. Sprinkle with 1 teaspoon mace and stir in 1 teaspoon vanilla. Pour over peaches. Bake in very hot oven (450 degrees) for 10 minutes, then reduce heat to 350 degrees and bake 40-50 minutes or until knife comes out clean. Sprinkle confectionery sugar on top of the filling and cool.

Grandma's Peach Jam

Have ready 1 quart of apple juice in a large jelly kettle, add sliced peaches to cover the apple juice. Add 1 dozen peach seeds. Cook all together and mash. Measure and for every cup of apple-peach mixture, add 1 cup of sugar. Cook slowly stirring often till reduced in half. Bottle and seal. This is how we still make peach jam, except we now make some into freezer jam. Follow the directions on the pectin of your choice.

Flamed Peach

In a pan, put 1/4 cup butter and melt slowly on low heat. Add 1 quart of your most flavorful peaches, peeled and chopped. Sprinkle with 1 cup sugar. Gently saute, stirring, and sprinkle 1 teaspoon mace over. Turn up the heat and pour over 1/4 cup peach brandy, flame. Arrange peach halves around a pretty dish and add a scoop of ice cream. After eating this you will know why I included these wild peach recipes.

Pickled White Cling Peaches

Wash and peel your peaches. Stick 3 whole cloves into each peach. Cover with a pickle solution of 1 cup vinegar and 2 cups sugar, heated and dissolved. Pack peaches into a jar and add 1 stick cinnamon to each quart. Cover with vinegar-sugar solution. Put lids on and sit aside a week or so. Then they are ready to eat.

Wild Grapes (Vitis spp.) grow extensively in many parts of the country. In the South they have muscadines, but here in West Virginia they are a smaller relative. They are good for eating out of hand. I pick them when they first ripen in the fall. These are picked off, washed and placed in freezer containers. I can then eat them raw or make my juice, preserves or ketchup. The grapes should be picked as soon as they ripen. As they age, then begin to dry and wrinkle. These grapes also make fine wine. One can find fallen wild grapes on top of the snow in the middle of winter. These are used extensively by the wild animals and birds. The grape leaf should be picked earlier in the season but my Grandmother Elsie gathered the leaf and fruit at the same time and packed them alternately with sugar to keep all winter long.

Wild Grape
Vitis riparia

A pie can be made by popping the hulls and using for filling. Some folks make jelly. Any grapes I have gathered are used in the recipes given here. I prefer my jelly and pies be made with something else beside grapes. Lest you forget, all these wild foods are very time consuming.

Wild Grape Preserves

Pick off and wash the tiny grapes. Just cover with water and cook. Pass through a foley mill to get the pulp. Mix 1/2 cup sugar for each cup of this pulp. Cook slowly, stirring now and then until it is thick. When done, add 1 teaspoon butter to each cup and sprinkle with cinnamon, if you like.

Wild Grape Juice

I make this usually to extend what cultivated grape juice I use. It can be used alone but I never have enough of either for my winter use. By using my tomato, rhubarb and other berries I have my year's supply of juice. Cook grapes in water and place in a jelly bag to drip over night. Place in jars, seal and cook in a hot water bath for 30 minutes.

Wild Grape Ketchup

Prepare the grapes as you did for preserves and to each cup of puree add 1/2 cup brown sugar, 1/4 cup grape wine vinegar, 1/2 teaspoon black pepper and 1 teaspoon spicewood berries that have been ground. Cook until thickened and add your spices last. This is especially good with fowl but can be used with any meat. I prefer it rather than cranberries.

Wild Grape Salad

Have puree made and ready. Take 1 1/2 cups water, heat to boiling with one tablespoon fresh thyme or 1/4 teaspoon dried. Keep the pan covered, remove from the heat for thyme to steep. Soften two packages plain gelatin in 1/2 cup of water. Strain thyme from the water and re-heat, if necessary. Stir in the softened gelatin then add 2 cups grape puree. Place in refrigerator until partly jelled. Sir in 2 cups finely chopped celery and the juice of a lemon. Pour in prepared mold and chill. When ready to serve, turn out and garnish with cream cheese frosting (see below) or sour cream.

Wild Grape Dessert Jello

Make the same as the salad grape jello. Leave out the thyme and celery. I sometimes use pears in this, but mostly I fold in whipped cream.

Wild Cherries

Wild cherries (prunus spp.), one kind or another, grow from Canada to Georgia and West to Kansas. You will have to have more time than anything else to preserve wild cherries. The easiest way I know is to pick, wash and package for freezer and do what you want in the winter when time is more available. Mostly, I eat these straight from the freezer. Scout out your tree when they are ripe, some will be larger and better tasting than others. I have wild cherry trees at the end of the driveway. One has cherries about half the size of a regular cherry and the other is about half the size of my tree, too small and bitter to use. I have no idea why this is. The trees being so close, one would think the cherries produced would be the same, but not so. The wild animals and birds make good use of this food. Even my dogs chomp away on ones that fall to the ground in the Fall. If you want to use them other than raw, here's how. Remember peach and cherry pits contain a poison.

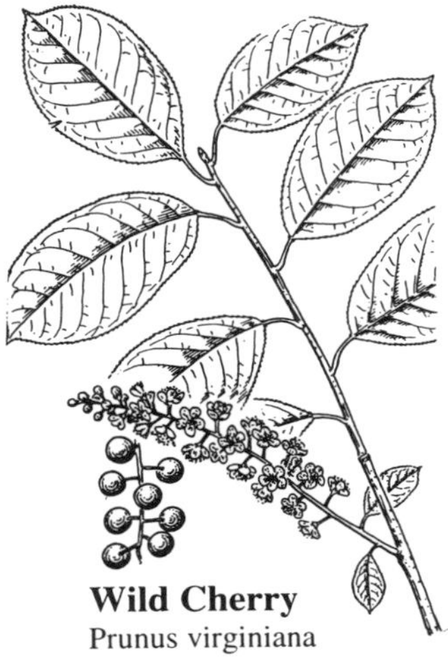

Wild Cherry
Prunus virginiana

Wild Cherry Jelly

Wash and clean 4 cups of cherries, add to 4 cups boiling water, remove to cool. Drain and run cherries through colander to remove seeds. I tried my foley mill and it did a pretty fair job. I would think a Squeezo might work better. Let set overnight, in the morning pour off the top water, down to the thick pulp. To 2 3/4 cups of this pulp, add 1/4 cup lemon juice. Mix and stir in 5 cups white sugar. Bring to a rolling boil. Add 1 pouch Certo and stir. Bring back to a rolling boil and boil 1 minute. Makes 5 pints.

Wild Cherry Pie

Mix 2 cups wild cherry juice, 3 tablespoons cornstarch and 1/2 cup white sugar. Stir to a boil. Add 1/8 teaspoon almond flavoring when finished cooking. pour into a cornflake pie shell and cool. Top with whipped cream and decorate with maraschino cherries.

Wild Cherry Syrup or Drink

Make a batch of the cherries for juice and pulp, sweeten, cold pack 20 minutes. Now, for syrup, use as it or, for a drink, pour glass 1/3 full of the syrup then fill up with ice cubes and gingerale.

Wild Cherry Jello Mold

Mix 4 cups of the cherry pulp, sweetened to taste, and 2 envelopes plain gelatin. Make as any jello, let set till syrupy and fold in 1 cup whipped topping and 1 cup finely chopped hickory nuts. Place in pretty individual molds. Unmold in a cloud of the whipped topping or ice cream. Garnish with white grapes.

Wild Persimmon (Diospyros virginiana) grows almost over the entire United States. They grow both wild and cultivated. The cultivated persimmon is huge compared to the wild ones. They can be purchased, October through the Winter months, in some grocery stores. These are a beauty to behold and have no seeds. If you don't have excesses of the wild ones, do get acquainted with the other ones. You might just be glad you did.

Wild Persimmon
Diospyros virginiana

Finding a nice tree laden with fruit on a cold Fall day is indeed a treat. They are ripe when wrinkled, brownish and gooey. If they are smooth and a pretty orange, leave them where they are. There is nothing quite like the supreme bitter taste of biting into a nice plump orange unripe persimmon. Contrary to popular belief it does not have to frost or freeze for the fruit to be ripe. They ripen from late Fall into Winter and fall when completely ripe. All the freezing and thawing in the world will not ripen your persimmon if picked before ripened. The wild animals feed heavily on the fruits as they fall to the ground, so much so you may have trouble getting enough for yourself. Some trees are better and larger, so scout out your tree and stake your claim. A few strands of cotton thread around and over the under growth should take care of the animals.

The best way to gather these 'simmons is to spread a sheet of cloth or plastic under the tree and shake. Only the ripe ones will fall. Pick them up, wash and mash. I prepare quite a batch this way and put the pulp in freezer containers for use all year. The cap is tough and resembles a strawberry cap. This needs to be sliced off with a knife.

The cap tries to pull all the seeds out, all six of them. I cover them with cold water and wash and cap. When I have 12 cups washed and capped, I add 4 cups of cold water. Mash with a potato masher. Push down and pull up and push down. You will never get all the pulp off those seeds. Now fill your foley food mill and push the pulp out. The pulp will be nice and dark orange. This is either used now or frozen. Any cooking will turn this darker brown and toughen the fibers. If you are using the pulp in a raw stage, it needs to be consumed soon for the longer it sits the darker it gets. It's great in ice cream or chiffon pie. I tried to make persimmon butter and the longer it cooked the darker and tougher it got. It is edible but sure not butter and you could not spread it at all. The chickens thought it was wonderful! So it goes when working with wild things. Some of my recipes were not good at all and some were surprisingly good. What follows is the good ones.

Persimmon leaves may the gathered early in the year to dry for tea. Gather them when the leaves are fully developed and still full of sap--before they start to turn color in the fall. Store some away to enjoy all year long.

Wild Persimmon Drop Cookies

1 cup sugar	1/2 teaspoon allspice
1/2 cup butter	2 cups self rising flour
1 beaten egg	1 cup persimmon pulp
1/2 teaspoon cinnamon	1 cup black walnuts
1/2 teaspoon cloves	1 cup finely chopped dried apples

Cream the sugar and butter. Add the beaten eggs. Stir in the persimmon pulp with the sifted dry ingredients. Fold in the dried apples and walnuts that have been dusted with flour. Drop by teaspoon onto a well greased and floured cookie sheet. Bake in a 350 degree oven for about 15 minutes or until soft to touch but done. Enjoy with a nice cup of simmon leaf tea anytime.

Baked Wild Persimmon Pie

Sift together:

- 1 cup flour
- 3/4 cup sugar
- 1/4 teaspoon baking powder
- 1/4 teaspoon salt

Stir in:

- 1 beaten egg
- 2 cup persimmon puree
- 1/3 cup milk
- 1 teaspoon powdered ginger

Mix all well and pour into the pie shell. Bake at 350 degrees for 30 minutes or until a toothpick inserted in the middle comes out clean. Sprinkle the top with cookie crumbs or hickory nuts (finely chopped). Cool. Serve with whipped ricotta cheese.

Ricotta Cheese Topping

1 cup ricotta cheese, whipped with 1/2 cup sugar and 1 teaspoon vanilla. Add milk 1 tablespoon at a time, to get the correct consistency.

Wild Persimmon Chiffon Pie

- 1 graham cracker crust
- 3 cups persimmon pulp
- 2 packages gelatin
- 1 tablespoon rum extract
- 1/2 cup warm water
- 1 cup whipping cream

Soften the gelatin in the water and add the honey. Place in a double boiler to heat. Stir to dissolve. Remove from the heat and cool slightly. Stir in persimmon pulp and rum extract. When completely cold, stir in the whipped cream. Pour into the graham cracker crust and refrigerate several hours. Garnish with whipped cream before serving.

Wild Persimmon Ice Cream

1/2 cups persimmon puree	1 cup sugar
3 beaten eggs	1 1/2 cups evaporated milk
1 teaspoon orange extract	1 orange zest and juice

Beat the eggs and sugar. Grate orange peel and remove the juice. Stir this into the persimmon puree than into the milk, sugar and eggs. Add extract and freeze in an ice cream maker. Makes 1 quart.

Wild Persimmon Cake

1 cup persimmon pulp	1/2 cup sugar
1 tablespoon butter	1 cup self-rising flour
1/2 teaspoon salt	

Cream the butter and sugar. Stir in the pulp. Sift the dry ingredients and stir them in. Beat well. Pour into a well greased and floured Bundt pan. Bake at 350 degrees for 40 minutes or until a toothpick inserted comes out clean. Frost with your favorite frosting or the one that follows.

Boiled Frosting

Mix 3 tablespoons flour with 1 cup milk. Cook in double boiler till thick. Cool. Cream 1 cup butter with 1 cup sugar and add to the milk mixture. Beat well and add 1 teaspoon rum extract last. Frost your cake.

Steamed Wild Persimmon Pudding

Beat together:

1 cup persimmon pulp	1 cup sugar
1 tablespoon rum	1 beaten egg
2 tablespoons melted shortening	

Add sifted together:

1 cup self-rising flour	1 teaspoon cinnamon
1/2 teaspoon salt	

Add to the above:

1/2 cup buttermilk that has 1 teaspoon soda stirred in.

Mix all together and pour into a well-greased one pound coffee can or mold. Have steaming pot boiling. Set in pan on a rack in the boiling water. Fill with more boiling water till the water height equals the batter height. Put on the lit and simmer for two hours. Do not remove the lid for a peek. Remove, let cool and turn out from the mold. Serve with lemon curd or hard sauce.

Lemon Curd

1 lemon	1/3 cup sugar
1 tablespoon butter	1 egg

Fill a double boiler with enough water to bring it to the bottom of (and touching) the top boiler. Heat the bottom boiler water to boiling. Rub the inside of the top pan with the butter and place on top. Now add the sugar, juice and zest of one lemon. Stir to heat and dissolve the sugar. Add the beaten egg and stir gently, in one direction around the pan till the mixture is a clear, pale yellow. Cool.

Quick Simmon Loaf

2 cups persimmon pulp	1/4 pound butter
1 cup sugar	2 beaten eggs
1 3/4 cups self rising flour	1/4 cup hickory nuts

Cream butter and sugar. Stir in pulp. Add beaten eggs, then the flour. Beat well. Stir in the nuts. Pour in to a large loaf pan. Bake at 350 degrees for 45 minutes. Test with a toothpick before removing from the oven to be sure it is done. I also use this recipe for breakfast muffins and serve warm with honey butter.

Wild Persimmon Vinegar

Take all your leftover seed-pulp mixture and place in a clean five-gallon container. If you are using plastic, make sure the bucket is a food grade. If you are using a crock, wash well and rinse out all the soap residue. Place in the sun to sterilize. Never use anything metal about any fermenting foods. Cover the pulp-seed mixture with water. Stir with a wooden paddle every day for a week. Then let set 2 more weeks. Strain out the seeds and place in gallon jugs with lids on loosely for about 6 months or longer. Your vinegar will produce a milky scum called "mother." It is a necessary part of the vinegar. When this falls to the bottom, usually your vinegar is done. Strain the vinegar again to get the mother out. Place in clean bottles and it's ready to use. I don't strain out the mother till I'm ready to use this vinegar. I used 5 gallon of the persimmons when writing this and came out with 2 gallons of vinegar.

Since I make several vinegars, I label and date the jugs and just let them set in the cellar. Some vinegars will take a year to be finished. Homemade vinegars are usually higher in acid content than store-bought ones so you may need to add a little water when using. Let your taste be your guide.

Pawpaw (Asimina triloba) is known as the West Virginia banana. I understand that whatever State it is grown in, it is automatically known as the State's wild banana. This has always grown near a creek at my grandmother's farm. I have tried to transplant it many times with no luck. I have also planted the seeds, no luck there either. I have covered quite a lot of acres over the years and that is the only place I have ever seen it growing. It is a small tree with a fruit of green about 4 inches long and 1 1/2 thick. The custard-like pulp has an odd flavor like nothing else I've known. It was often used and eaten raw. It has large oblong brown seeds that are poison. It is said the seeds should not dry out, but be planted directly in the ground. I tried this, but I still don't have any paw paw growing on my farm. The fruit does not keep well. It is better to pick them green and let them ripen until soft and brown. As is true with most wild fruits, eat them as soon as they ripen. If you want to cook them, here are a few recipes you can try.

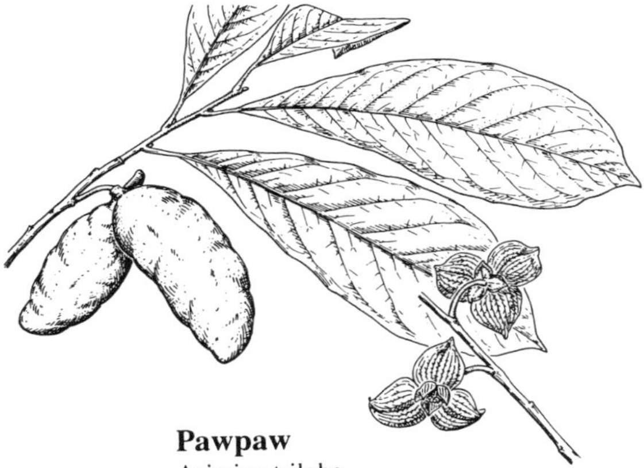

Pawpaw
Asimina triloba

Pawpaw Pudding

2 cups mashed pawpaws
2 teaspoons powdered ginger
1 teaspoon cinnamon
1/2 teaspoon nutmeg
1/2 cup milk
1/2 cup honey
3/4 cup sugar

Mix in order given. Beat well. Pour into a prepared pan and bake 1 hour at 350 degrees.

Pawpaw Bars

1 cup pawpaws mashed
1 1/4 cup white sugar
2 cups self-rising flour
1 cup melted shortening
4 eggs beaten
1 tablespoon lemon extract

Cream the shortening and sugar together. Stir in the mashed paw paws, eggs and lemon extract. Fold in the flour and beat well. Turn dough into a prepared pan and bake 350 degrees for 30 minutes. Cool while preparing the frosting.

Pawpaw Bars Frosting

2 1/2 cups confectionery sugar
1 tablespoon powdered dry lemon peel
1 teaspoon lemon extract

Add small amounts of water at a time to mix, just enough to reach spreading consistency. Spread on the bars. Cool and cut into squares.

Pawpaw Cookies

1 cup pawpaw pulp	1 teaspoon soda
1 cup chopped hickory nuts	1 cup currents
1 cup sugar	1 teaspoon mace
1 egg beaten	2 cups flour
1/2 cup butter or lard (no substitutes)	1/2 teaspoon salt

Cream sugar and shortening of choice. Mix soda with paw paw pulp and mix in the sugar mixture. Add the beaten egg. Beat well with each addition. Stir in the sifted flour, salt and mace. Sometimes, I don't add any seasoning except 1/2 teaspoon salt, so the flavor comes through clear and pronounced. Drop by spoonful onto prepared cookie sheet. Bake at 350 degrees for about 15 minutes.

Pawpaw Coffee Cake

1/2 cup shortening	1 1/2 cup sugar
2 eggs beaten	2 cups self-rising flour
3/4 teaspoon soda	1/2 cut buttermilk
1 cup peeled and mashed pawpaw	Rum

Cream shortening with sugar. Beat in eggs and seasoning. Stir the soda into the buttermilk and stir with the flour. Pour into a prepared baking pan. Bake at 350 degrees for about an hour or until a toothpick inserted comes out clean. I like to glaze this by melting 1/4 lb. butter, adding 1 cup water, 1 cup sugar and boil for 5 minutes. Stir in rum and brush evenly over the cooled cake. Sprinkle with hickory nuts, if you like, but not necessary.

Quince

A Quince is a fruit tree that grows in much of the United States. It has been nearly forgotten. In all my seed catalogs, I can find no quince tree, but it should be remembered and as much used today as in yesteryear.

Quince Butter

Wash, but don't peel. Slice and remove seeds. Cook with small amount of water. Cook until tender. Run through a foley mill. To each cup of quince puree, add one cup of water and 1 cup sugar. Place in crock pot and stir till sugar dissolves. Cook till thick and dark red. Place in sterilized jar and seal. Process in hot water bath for 15 minutes.

Quince Jelly

Wash; peel if using for more than jelly. Remove seeds and slice thin. They require a lot of cooking to make them tender. You could just use the peeling for jelly and make butter or preserves from the slices. They can also be extended with the addition of apple peels (red) for jelly. About half quince and half apple. Pour into a jelly bag and hang to drain over night. To each cup of juice, use 2/3 cup sugar. Stir to dissolve sugar and continue to boil until mixture sheets from a spoon. If you want, use a gel. Follow apple jelly directions included on the pectin box. Place in hot sterilized jars and seal.

Candied Quince

Wash, peel, remove seeds and slice the quince thin. Simmer in a small amount of water until tender. Remove slices and measure the liquid. To each cup of liquid, add 2 cups white sugar and 1/3 cup light corn syrup. Boil this until it reaches 234 degrees on candy thermometer or until it spins a thread. Have the quince slices well drained and place carefully into the syrup leaving plenty of space as not to crowd them. Cook until clear, skimming the froth from the syrup. Place on a screen and dry.

Quince Jam or Honey

Wash, peel, core and chop fine 5 lbs. quinces. Put the peels and core on to cook separately and simmer until cooked through. Strain off the juice from these and add the chopped quinces. Keep the whole quinces in cold water till time to chop and put into the hot peeling juice. Cook the quince till tender. Drain off the juice. Mix 4 cups of this with 6 cups pure sugar and boil this to get a syrup. Pour into sterilized jars and process in hot water bath for 15 minutes. Quince is a very rich jam and if you are short of quinces, pears or sweet apples can be substituted in the recipe. Other fruits were often used to make more quince. This jam was made often to fill Grandma's cookie jar with her filled cookies.

Baked Quince

Have a prepared casserole dish with lid and heat oven to 325 degrees. Wash, peel, core and quarter quince. Allow at least one for each person, plus one for the pot. Place water in casserole to 1/4 inch. Add in 6-7 quince and sprinkle with 1 cup sugar. Place on cover and bake about 2 hours or until tender and a pretty red. Serve warm with ice cream. They can be stewed on top of the stove, but will need more water to cook.

Filled Cookies with Qunice Jam or Quince Honey

2 cup sugar
2 eggs beaten
2 teaspoons baking powder
1 teaspoon lemon extract
1 cup butter
1 teaspoon salt
1 teaspoon soda dissolved in 1 cup sour milk
6+ cups of all purpose flour sifted

Cream sugar and butter. Add beaten eggs. Combine dry ingredients. Sift and add alternately with the milk to the first mixture. Add the lemon extract. Add more flour to make workable dough. Divide this into 3 equal parts. Let set to rest a few hours, but not overnight. Roll 1/4 inch thick. Cut with a large cookie cutter. I use 1 lb. coffee can. Place jam in one-half and fold over. Moisten edges and seal. Bake at 375 degrees for about 20 minutes.

Quince Turnover

2 cup flour
1 teaspoon salt
1/3 cup shortening
Ice water

Cut shortening into flour and salt. Add just enough ice water to make stiff dough. Cut in half and roll out on floured board. Cut out circles with a 1 lb. coffee can. Place a bit of the quince jam to one side. Moisten the edges and fold over. Press to seal. Place on a well-oiled cookie sheet and bake. This recipe can also be used for fried pies. These were almost always baked.

Quince Squares

2 cups self-rising flour sifted
1 egg beaten
2 tablespoons cooking oil
1 cup milk

Mix together. Add 1 cup of any of the quince preserves. Beat well. Pour into a buttered and floured 9x9 inch baking pan. Bake at 350 degrees for 30 minutes or until testing done. Cool. Cut into bars. Serve with ice cream and spread quince jelly over all.

Quince Pudding

2 cups flour	2 teaspoons butter
2 teaspoons baking powder	1 egg
1/2 teaspoon salt	1 cup milk
1 cup quince preserves	Flavoring

Mix. Add preserves and flavoring last. Bake at 350 degrees for 30 minutes. Cut into squares. Serve with whipped cream.

Stuffed Quince

Wash and core as many quince as you need. Place in a deep dish with 2 cups sugar and water to nearly cover. Fill center with raisins. Bake till tender and some of the water has evaporated into a syrup. Cool. Fill with whipped cream and drizzle with syrup.

Wild Strawberries (Fragaria spp.) are also fruits for the gods. I grew up on these things, but many have never tasted them. I am so sorry for them. These grew readily in the fields and the best were usually found on the edge of the woods. We picked them by the stem which holds several berries in different degrees of ripeness. It took little effort to pick a water bucket full of these stems, and you just knew there would be strawberry shortcake for supper. When you got home, the effort for that shortcake was more 'cause they all had to be capped one tiny berry at a time. After all were capped, sugar was added, and they were placed in the cellar till supper when Mom would fire up the wood range and bake the shortcake. The berries were then put in between and all over the top while the shortcake was still warm. That was supper, usually all you could eat of strawberry shortcake and milk dip. Recipe follows. If no wild strawberries are to be had, try cultivated ones.

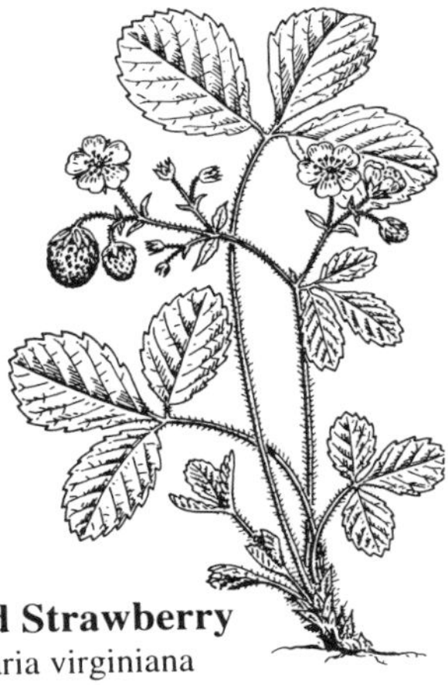

Wild Strawberry
Fragaria virginiana

Wild Strawberry Shortcake

3 cups all-purpose flour
3/4 cup butter
3/4 cup milk
1 tablespoon baking powder
1/4 cup sugar

Mix dry ingredients and cut in the butter. Then fold in the milk gently. Refrigerate about 1 hour. Have oven hot (400 degrees) and a pan greased and ready. Divide dough in half. Roll to about 1/2 inch thick. Place one in bottom of pan and butter the top. Now, place other rolled 1/2 piece over the first. Bake. Remove from oven and lift off top. have prepared your wild strawberries that have been sugared. You will need about 2 quarts for this size shortcake. Place 1/2 of the berries on the bottom shortcake and then put on the top. Cover with berries and let the juice flow over the sides. This was always served with a rich milk dip.

Milk Dip

To 1 quart of Half and Half milk add 1 or more cups of sugar (this depended on which Grandma was making it). Stir until dissolved. Pour over your piece of the shortcake, either a little or a lot. This milk dip was used over rolls, cobblers and dumplings of all kinds.

Wild Blackberry (Rubus spp.)of several varieties grow wild everywhere in West Virginia. They range from a small seedy berry called "ewe teats" and left to the birds, to long shiny sweet juicy berries that are picked for canning, jelly, jam, wine, pies, cakes and cobblers. When I was small I can remember going to the back field where those long black shiny ones grew. We took along our lunch of homemade bread and cucumber sandwiches.

We carried a washtub with everyone having a small pail to pick in and pour into the tub. Mom and all the children spent the day pickin' berries. Then we had to carry that tub home where it was placed in the cool cellar till morning. A cobbler with plenty of rich milk was supper. Then the next day they were worked up or made into jelly, jam and jars canned for our winter food. Many cold winter suppers were simply a jar of canned blackberries poured over crumbled homemade bread and with lots of good milk. Doesn't sound like much of a supper in today's world but we all grew up rather healthy. Today I freeze most of the berries for pies, etc. Also, I use Sure-Jell cooked on an electric stove but Mom did all of hers on a wood cooking stove and no Sure-Jell in the jelly or jam either. It had to be cooked a long time and sometimes it was too thin or too runny but we ate it anyway.

Blackberry
Rubus rose

Wild Blackberry Cake

- 1 cup shortening
- 3 eggs
- 2 teaspoons cinnamon
- 1 teaspoon nutmeg
- 1/2 cup juice
- 1/2 cup sour milk
- 1/2 cup warm water
- 2 cups sugar
- 1 cut raw berries
- 1 teaspoon cloves
- 2 1/2 cups flour
- 1/2 teaspoon salt
- 2 teaspoons soda

Cream shortening and sugar and add the beaten eggs. Add berries, juice, sour milk and spices. Add flour and warm water that the 2 teaspoons soda has been dissolved in. Bake 350 degrees for about 1 hour. This was my Grandmother's recipe. It was also cooked on a wood stove. She always made Boiled Frosting for this.

Boiled Frosting

Boil 1/2 cup water with 1 cup sugar till the hard crack stage or 244 degrees on a candy thermometer. Beat 2 egg whites till they peak. Slowly add the syrup all the while beating the egg whites.

Boiled Wild Blackberry Dumplin'

Dumplings--

- 1 cup flour
- 2 1/2 tablespoons butter
- 1 teaspoon baking powder
- 1 teaspoon salt
- 1 1/2 cup sugar
- Milk for dropping batter

Sauce--

- 4 cups blackberries
- 1 cup water
- 1 cup sugar

Put sauce ingredients into a wide bottom pan. Stir to boil. Make dumplin' mix. Pour this by spoonful over the blackberry mixture. Put on the lid and do not remove until cooked, about 20 minutes.

Wild Blackberry Roll

2 cups flour	1/2 cup butter
2 tablespoon sugar	1 teaspoon salt
1 tablespoons baking powder	3/4 cup milk

Sift dry ingredients together and cut in the butter. Add milk and mix quickly. Don't handle the dough any more then necessary. Roll out about 1/4 to 1/2 inch thick. Cover with the berries. Roll up jelly roll fashion. Place in a well greased pan. Pour over the syrup. Bake 400 degrees for 30-35 minutes. Slice and serve with dip, whipped or ice cream. See raspberry syrup or use a simple syrup.

Berry Filling--2 cups any berries dusted with 1/4 cup flour and 1/2 cup sugar.

Syrup-- Boil together 2 cups sugar and 2 cups water and 1 tablespoon butter.

Wild Blackberry Pie

Pastry for 2-crusts pie. Mix 3 cups fresh berries with 1 cup sugar, 4 tablespoons tapioca (quick cooking). Place in bottom shell. Dot with 2 tablespoons butter. Cover with top crust and seal edges. Brush top with milk and bake at 400 degrees for 10 minutes. Reduce heat to 350 degrees for 20 minutes.

Wild Raspberry (Rubus spp.) can be used in the blackberry recipes but after a cobbler or just freshly eaten, I usually make raspberry vinegar, syrup or jam. Everyone will have their own preferences, so experiment to find what you like best.

Raspberry
Rubus occidentalis

Wild Raspberry Syrup

To 4 cups berries, add 4 cups sugar and 3 cups water. Stir and simmer 15 minutes. Strain and bottle juice. I usually put the leftover pulp in a pan, spread thin and make a leather. This can be used in mincemeat, cookies, cakes or just as a chewy snack or add to a bird feed cake. The syrup is super over ice cream. A nice drink is made by using 1/3 glass syrup and fill with club soda and ice cubes. The children will enjoy 1/3 glass syrup, 1/3 milk and the remainder filled with ice milk.

Wild Raspberry Vinegar

To 9 cups raspberries, add enough water to just cover. Add 1 cup sugar. Stir and mash up the berries. Pour into a sterilized gallon glass jug. Do not seal, but cover with a cloth held in place by a rubber band. Let this set until you see a jelly-like mass in the jug. This is called "mother" and is important to make your vinegar. When it tastes as you like, strain off the vinegar, bottle, and cork. I usually make it this year to be used next year. Herbs may be used in this, but I usually leave my raspberry vinegar as is and add herbs to the apple vinegar. These make beautiful gifts.

Wild Huckleberries (Vaccinium spp.) must be fruits for the gods. So small, hard to pick and clean but the effort will be all worth it. It is getting almost impossible to forage these because the wild animals, especially the deer and turkey, like them so well. At one time, morning pickin' of huckleberries would produce a water bucket full. Now, I must figure a morning will produce about a pint or so of berries. All that is left are a few berries on the underneath of the bushes. I have tried digging them and putting them closer to the house with no luck. If I'm not very careful, the deer come into my yard and the turkey come very close too.

I have devised my own way to dissuade these wild animals from eating me out of house and home. Take a roll of cotton thread and drape it over the bushes. You can put short stakes in the ground and run it around them. You need to start about blooming time and you will need to check them about once a week. The string will need to be raised as the grasses grow. You want that string visible and just topping the vegetative growth. It seems they are afraid of catching their feet in this. I have done this several years in the garden, and it has worked for deer, rabbit and turkey. I don't know about the woodchuck, but it will probably work for them too, or a version of this string will. It doesn't work for chipmunk. They go right under it and remove any and all seeds. After planting my beans three times, I figured out how to outsmart those things. After planting and covering my seeds, I take a length of string about 3 times the length of the row to be protected and lay it in a snake-like pattern the length of the row. When the plants come up, I then put in short stakes with the string in a zig-zag fashion for the other animals. The birds will not frequent your garden if the string is too high from the ground and some will not ever go in. I either put up with this string

Huckleberry
Vaccinium vacillans

system or lose it all to the critters. So, if I'm having huckleberries, that is how I'm going to have to do it.

What few huckleberries I can get will go in my favorite dessert. They can be canned, dried and made into jam. Huckleberries make a most delicious syrup for pancakes and ice cream.

Wild Huckleberry Syrup

Combine 4 cups each of berries, sugar and water. Boil together and strain. Add the zest and juice of a lemon or 3 tablespoons of berry vinegar. Reheat and seal. Place in a hot water bath and boil 10 minutes.

Mom's Wild Huckleberry Rolls

Make your favorite 2 crust pie doughs rolled into 8 rounds. 4 cups huckleberries dusted with 1 cup of sugar and 1/2 cup flour. Put 1/2 cup of the berries in the center of each pie crust dough. Dot with 1 teaspoon butter. Bring up each side of pastry to form a half moon and seal edges. Now, set in a butter-greased baking pan. Pour over this a sugar syrup made from 1 cup sugar and I cup water. Bake 375 at degrees for 30-40 minutes. Serve cold or cool with ice cream. This recipe came from the Shuttlesworth or my Mother's side of the family. I have never heard of anyone else making these rolls, but they sure are memories for me.

Wild Huckleberry continued

Mom's Wild Huckleberry Jam

Use 1 quart of cleaned huckleberries. These should be a bit under-ripe if possible as they will jell better. 1 quart of cleaned and chopped very green apples, don't peel or core. Cook in as little amount of water as possible. Strain off the apple juice and pour over the berries. Add equal amount of white sugar to the amount of apple juice and berries. Cook stirring often until thick. Now days you open a box of Sure-Jell and follow the recipe for the blueberries. This jam is very iffy--If the apples were green enough and the berries under ripe, you could get a nice jam. If not it was too thin. If Mom had a lemon, the problem would have been corrected.

Mulberry

Native mulberry, commonly called the Red Mulberry (Morus rubra), is really purplish when ripe and is a much-neglected fruit growing extensively over most of the United States. The young shoots and just-forming leaves make a nice pot herb. Wash and cook until tender and serve up with butter, a sprinkle of salt and pepper. The fruits and leaves act as a laxative--purgative, in herbal medicine language. Jelly can be made from the fruit by cooking and straining. You will need to add an acid food with the juices as they have no pectin. Green apples or unripe blackberries will do, as will the juice of a lemon. The juice can be used as a cold drink as well.

Red Mulberry
Morus rubra

Mulberry Pie

A pie can be made by placing about 3 cups of the berries in an unbaked or partially baked crust. Mix 3/4 cup sugar with 1 tablespoon tapioca and sprinkle over the berries. You may want to add a bit of lemon juice and peel for seasoning. I have used cinnamon, but prefer just the berries. Cover with crust top and bake in a 450 degree oven for 10 minutes. Reduce heat to 350 degrees and cook 45 minutes. Cool and serve.

Mulberry continued

Dry the berries for winter use in place of raisins, but they are very seedy. The easiest way to obtain the berry is to place a sheet of plastic on the ground and shake the tree. Insects do not seem to bother with my tree but in some areas they do. Place in salt water and weigh the berries down with a plate. Let this set 30 minutes or so then remove plate and let a small stream of water flow in and over the pans edge to wash out the insects. Swish the berries around in your hand an pick over before using. You may also want to de-stem the berries by snipping off the stem with scissors, down to the berry. However, what is a little more roughage in your pie? Mulberries do not keep well after removing from the tree, so make something from them as soon as picked. For drying, pick and prepare in the early morning on a clear hot day. Place on a screen, cover with cheese cloth and put out in the hot sun. Preferably over a hot rock, concrete walk or a roof. Place cups or some such item under all four corners to keep air flowing under the screen. Bring in at night, stir and return to the sun in the morning. They should be considerably smaller now and if it is rainy, place in a warm 150 degree oven to finish drying. When completely dry, store in a glass jar covered and place in a dark cupboard. They can be used to extend blackberries.

Elderberries (Sambucus canadensis) is a low growing and spreading bush. It is a pretty shrub for garden or lawn. It is a useful food for humans as well as birds. The stem, root and leaf are poison but the flowers and berries are edible in several ways. In late June, a white flower head with tiny flowerets about the size of a saucer appears. It is now time to use the flowers. The flower heads can be made into wine, tea and fritters. Dry the flower heads intact for a winter tea. The way I use them most is for fritters. I have yet to ever find anyone who doesn't really like them. They are waited for with a great anticipation by several folks here about.

Elderberry
Sambucus canadensis

Elderberry Jelly

You can follow the direction on Sure-Jell or you can make it like I do. Gather 1 gallon wild apples and 1 quart or there about of elderberries. Wash and remove berries from the stems. Wash and quarter the apples, cutting out any bad places. Combine the apples and berries and cover with water. Cook till apples are tender. Drain out the juice over night in a jelly bag. Take 7 cups of this and mix with 1 package of Sure-Jell and the juice of 1 lemon. Stir until this comes to a full rolling boil. Add 9 cups of white sugar and return to a boil and boil 1 minute. Skim and place in hot sterilized jars. Process 10 minutes in hot water bath.

Elderberries alone are more or less an acquired taste. A true elderberry lover will not want anything added, even the lemon. I have never cared for them this way myself.

Elderflower Fritters

Gather the large flower heads intact. Check for insects, usually all you have to do is shoo away a bee or so. I do not wash these. Mix pancake batter as directed on the box except add a bit more liquid. Plunge one flower head in this batter and gently twirl it a bit. This is so all sides of the flowerets are covered with the pancake batter. Lift up and let drip a few seconds, now put in the hot fat to fry. I use corn oil to a depth of 2-3 inches in my electric skillet. I set the thermostat at 340 degrees. Let the fritter fry till brown and drain on paper. Now have a paper sack with powdered sugar and cinnamon ready. I use one teaspoon cinnamon to every cup of sugar. Place in your fritter and gently cover with the sugar mixture. Lift out, shake off excess sugar. Place on a plate and serve with some nice hot tea. I realize this sounds like a lot of work but it really isn't and so much worth the effort. This is one that my son and his friend expected early every summer, after a swim in the creek. If you never use elderberry any other way do try this just once.

Elderberry Pie

Use pastry for a two-crust unbaked pie. Set your oven at 375 degrees. Prepare filling with 3 1/2 cup cleaned, raw elderberries mixed with 1 cup white sugar and 3 tablespoons of tapioca. Pour into the shell and sprinkle with 1 teaspoon cinnamon and 2 tablespoons lemon juice. Cover with top. Cut slit to let the steam escape. Brush all over with milk and sprinkle with sugar. You can dry elderberries and use this recipe for the winter time, but, when I do, I like to add a peeled and sliced apple for they seem to be all seed after drying. I use dried elderberries in mince meat and fruit cakes.

Dried Elderberry Dumplings

These are often made in the winter. To 1 cup of dried elderberries add 2 cups water, 2 sliced apples, 1/2 cup sugar and 1 tablespoon butter. Simmer until apples are cooked. Add your dumplin' mix (see below), cover and do not remove lid for 20 minutes.

Drop Dumplings

1 cup self-rising flour
1/2 cup milk
3 tablespoons shortening.

Sprinkle with cinnamon and sugar. Serve either warm or cold.

Sumac

Staghorn sumac (Rhus typhina) is a beautiful small tree that grows in many places. It is as much of a bane to farmland as dandelions are to a lawn. The birds make good use of the berries. After cutting mine down last year, my bluebird population was way down this spring. I will not do that again, as one tree is not enough for the wildlife and me. In the spring, the sumac blooms a cone-shaped white flower head that is enjoyed by the bees.

Around August, the flower heads have develop-developed into a red cone of tiny velvety red berries. It is now time to enjoy the many foods of sumac. Select a tree where berries are short, fuzzy and look like red velvet. Pick what you need for your recipe. Leave others till you need them, as they don't keep well.

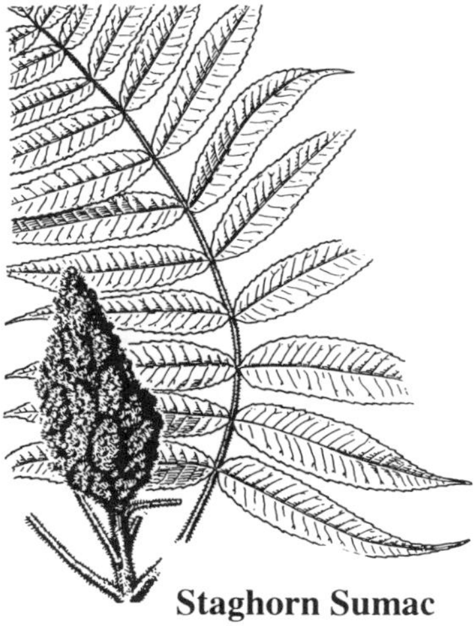

Staghorn Sumac
Rhus typhina

Pink Ade

Gather two sumac seed pods, wash and chop. Place in blender with cold water. Blend and let this set for about 30 minutes. Strain through cloth, three layers thick, to remove seeds and tiny hair. These hairs must be removed. This should make a quart or more depending on the size and age of the head. Add water and sweetener to taste.

Sumac Flammery

Start the same as for the ade. One head should make a pint of the juice, however, the age of the plant, where it is growing, when you pick it, all come into play and as does the weather. There are so many variables in using wild food. You will have to try and soon you will know the hows, how muchs and whys. Mix 1 cup sugar with 1 3/4 cup pink sumac ade. Put on high heat and bring to boil. Mix 1/4 cup ade with 3 tablespoons corn starch or arrowroot and stir into the sugar and ade. Stir until it returns to a full, rolling boil. Remove from fire and add 1 teaspoon butter, stirring to melt. Place in serving dishes and cool. Top with a dollop of whipped cream. This is very sweet dessert. You can cut back on the sugar if you prefer. I usually serve this with a lunch of wild salad greens when I want a small amount of a very sweet dessert. This is different and quite good!

Sumac Jelly

Start with 7 cups of the sumac ade made much stronger. Heat and re-strain. Place in a large pot and add 1 package of Sure-Jell. Bring to a boil, stirring till the boil cannot be stirred down. Have measured 9 cups of white sugar. Add slowly, but all at once, continuing to stir. Add 1 tablespoon of margarine. Continue stirring till, again, you get a boil you cannot stir down. Then, start counting this way: 1000-1, 1000-2, 1000-3, etc., till you have counted to1000-60. Remove from the heat. Have ready 12 half-pint jars. Add jelly mixture to jars. Seal. Place in hot water bath and process 15 minutes.

Pancake Jelly Roll

As a new bride many years ago, I could not get my jelly roll to come out right. Then I found this recipe. I have used it for years. It's easy and has never failed. It is a perfect accompaniment to my sumac jelly.

<u>Pancake Roll</u>
Beat 3 eggs until light and fluffy. Add 3/4 cup sugar and continue beating. Stir in 3 tablespoons melted butter and 1 teaspoon vanilla. Add 1 cup commercial pancake mix. Grease a shallow 10 x 15 inch pan and cover the bottom with wax paper that has been sprinkled with flour. Pour batter into pan and bake 10 minutes in a 400 degree oven. When done, immediately turn out on a clean towel or cloth that has been sprinkled with confectioners sugar. Roll the cloth and all. Let this cool, unroll, spread with jelly and then re-roll. Voila!

Sumac Syrup

Prepare one good size head of the sumac berry in 1 pint of cold water. Let this set about 30 minutes for flavors to enhance the water. Strain and mix ade with 2 cups white sugar. Heat, stir, boil 3 minutes. Again strain into syrup server. This will be a hit on any pancake. If you never try but one recipe for sumac, please try this just once!

Sumac Pie

Prepare 2 cups sumac ade. Mix with 1 cup sugar and 4 tablespoons corn starch. Stir and cook until clear. Cool. Then fold in whipped cream (please use the real thing). Pour into a graham cracker pie crust. I usually garnish this with a small pod-like piece of sumac seed head.

Ground Cherry is a member of the nightshade family. It grows on a two-foot sprawling bush with irregularly notched leaf. The flower is bell shaped, yellow with a dark center. It sets fruit with yellow berry enclosed in a five- sided paper husk. Let these husk fruit fall to the ground, as they will continue ripening. Green they are poison and at yellow greenish they don't taste good They need to be golden yellow. They will reach their full ripeness on the ground and can be gathered and stored in a cardboard box for eating all winter long. This is the way that I like them best and no work preserving them. They have a taste all their own, somewhat like a banana, pineapple, and fig all wrapped up in one tiny fruit. In growing them, use the same culture as tomatoes and remember tomato leaf and stems are also poison. Once you have developed a taste for ground cherry, they will always be something special.

Ground Cherry Filling

2 cups ground cherries	1/2 cup water
2/3 cup sugar	1 tablespoon tapioca
1 tablespoon butter	Juice of 1 lemon
1 teaspoon ginger	A double pie crust

Combine sugar and water, bring to a boil, dissolving sugar. Stir in ground cherries and tapioca. Cook, stirring five minutes. Remove from heat, add lemon juice and ginger. Place in unbaked pie shell and top. Bake 350 degrees for 30 minutes, or until crust is done.

Pie Crust

2 cups flour
1/2 teaspoon baking powder
1 teaspoon salt
1/3 cup boiling water
2/3 cup shortening

Sift dry ingredients. Pour boiling water over shortening, mix until creamy. Add the flour mixture and mix into a dough. Chill thoroughly (several hours). Makes one 9-inch double crust pie shell. I roll this between wax paper sheets and transfer to pie pan. Add top, moisten edges, crimp and prick top.

Honeyed Ground Cherries

1 cup ground cherries
1/4 cup honey
1 tablespoon lemon juice

Cook all together and serve with a nice muffin, toast; or, it is great on ice cream.

Ground Cherry Pudding Pie

1 cup self rising flour
2 tablespoon sugar
3/4 cup of water
3/4 cup solid shortening
1 egg
1 teaspoon vanilla
1 recipe for Ground Cherry Pie Filling

Combine flour and sugar. Cut in shortening. Add water and egg. Spread batter in 10-inch pie pan. Add the filling in the middle of this batter. Bake at 400 degrees for 30 to 40 minutes.

Filled Ground Cherry Cookies

2 1/4 cup sifted flour
2 teaspoon baking powder
1 cup sugar
1 teaspoon lemon extract
1/4 teaspoon salt
1/2 cup butter
2 eggs (beaten)
1 tablespoon molasses

Sift dry ingredients. Cream shortening, sugar and molasses. Add beaten eggs, then the dry ingredients. Use enough milk to cling everything together; add 1 tablespoon at a time. Work dough into a ball and let rest while you make your filling. Divide your dough into three pieces and roll. Cut with a round 3" cookie cutter. To half of these cookies place 1 teaspoon ground cherry filling. Top with the other half, moisten edge and crimp. Prick tops and bake at 375 degrees about 10 to 15 minutes.

Wild Nuts

Hickory Nuts

There are many species of hickory nuts but by far the best and easiest to harvest and crack are the shagbark (Carya ovata). Some hickory's don't produce nuts, but those that do are edible. As a child, I gathered these by the bucket and they were put to good use-- just about anywhere nuts were called for. Back in those days, there were no stores that stocked nuts. Now-a-days, nuts are so expensive, maybe you will want to harvest what is growing for free. The shellbark husks separate from the nut and fall free. All you have to do is pick them up and crack them.

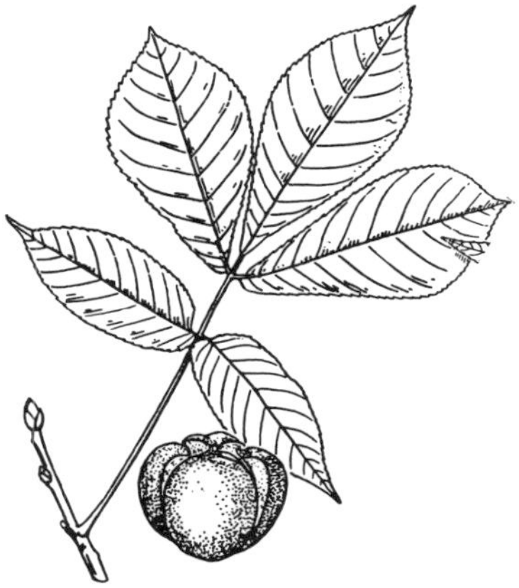

Shagbark Hickory
Carya ovata

Hickory Nut Pie

1 9-inch unbaked pie shell	3 eggs beaten
1/2 cup white sugar	1 cup light corn syrup
2 cups hickory nuts	1 teaspoon vanilla

Beat the eggs and sugar together. Mix in the corn syrup and vanilla. Beat well and fold in the hickory nuts. Pour in pie shell and bake 350 degrees for 30 minutes. Cool and serve.

Hickory Nut Cake

1 1/2 cups sugar — 2 cups sour cream
4 egg whites, beaten stiff — 3 cups flour, sifted
2 teaspoons soda dissolved in sour cream
1 teaspoon vanilla
1 teaspoon of baking powder sifted with flour
1 cup finely chopped nuts mixed with 1/2 cup of the flour

Add the sugar to the sour cream. Sift the flour and baking powder and add to the first mixture. Sir in the vanilla and nut-flour mixture. Fold in the stiffly beaten egg whites. Bake in a 350 degree oven about 35 minutes. Turn out on a rack to cool. Frost when cool.

This cake was often made on Saturday and served for Sunday dinner. It was always baked in a wood range. In the morning, it was my job to carry the wood and crack the nuts. A strong fire was going about 1 hour before the cake was mixed. Grandma passed her hand through the oven to see if it was hot enough and I kept the fire going. I was cautioned to be careful and not bang or drop anything as this would make her cake fall and it would be ruined. Saturday was also the day she had to kill, pick the feathers off and do the chicken for Sunday dinner. She probably made pies too or some other confectionery for Sunday dinner. Vegetables had to be gathered from the garden. Saturday was also cleaning day. There were also animals to feed, cows to milk and children to care for. She was mother to eleven children and reared 2 grandsons. How ever did she do all this? Come Sunday, my grandparents expected a house full of folks for dinner after church. I guess they averaged about 30 every Sunday! In those days, the older folks sat at the first table, the middle-aged folks ate next, then it was the children's turn. We very often ate mutton with that chicken and by that time, it was getting pretty cold and the fat stuck to the roof of your mouth. We were taught to respect our elders by calling them "Mr.and Mrs." and saying "Thank You," "Yes, Sir" and "No, Ma'am." So, if all this foraging seems like work, it is, but work is good for both body and soul, not even counting the money it saves.

Hickory Nut Rolls

Dough --
- 1 cake yeast
- 1/2 lb. margarine
- 1/2 lb. butter
- 1 pint sour cream
- 1/4 cup warm water
- 6 or more cups of flour
- 6 eggs separated

Dissolve the yeast in the warm water. Separate the eggs and mix the shortening with the yolk. Mix the flour into the egg shortening mixture. Add the cream and yeast water mixture. Knead all of this together. Roll this dough thin and cover with the beaten egg whites. Fold dough over and over to mix in the egg whites. Cover and let set to rise over night in a cool place, but not the refrigerator.

Filling--
- 2 cups cracked, picked over and crushed hickory nuts
- 2 cups white sugar
- 1 teaspoon vanilla
- Milk to make a stiff paste

Divide dough into 4 to 6 pieces for rolling dough very thin into a circle. Spread on nut paste and cut into wedges like a pie. The large side of the wedge should not be over 2 inches wide. Slit the peak about 1/2 inch and roll the dough up starting at the large end. Bake these 400 degrees for 15 to 20 minutes. Cool. Store in a container with a lid to let the flavors mingle. This makes a very big batch of cookies, but they won't last long once your family discovers them. I only make these at Christmas and sometimes split the filling recipe in half making some of them with walnuts.

Hickory Nut Brittle

Prepare 9x12 inch pyrex dish by buttering heavily. Spread 2 cups hickory nuts on bottom. Sprinkle with salt. Use a cast iron skillet or another heavy pan. Heat slowly 2 cups white sugar. Stir constantly till sugar is melted and turns a light brown color or when it reaches the hard crack stage. Pour the melted sugar over the nuts. Nuts and 9x12 inch dish should be warmed before adding the syrup. Cool. Break apart.

Bottom of the Barrel Candy

This candy was a combination of different kinds of the powdered nuts after pieces were used, like the bottom of the barrel nuts.

2 cups brown sugar 1/2 cup water
2 tablespoons butter
1 teaspoon mapeline flavoring
1/4 teaspoon broken nut meats

Boil the sugar and water to the stiff ball stage (246 degrees). Add the butter and cook until the brittle stage (290 degrees). Add the mapeline flavoring. Pour over the nut meats that have been placed in a warm 9x12 inch buttered dish. Cool and break into pieces.

Hazelnuts (Corylus spp.) are the first nuts most folks go to gather. Often, mine have all been picked when I get there. They are easy to pick from low growing bushes, easy to crack and nicely flavored. These nuts can be used in most any recipe calling for nuts, but they don't give the same flavor at all. Mostly, in my area, they are eaten out of hand and other nuts are used for cooking.

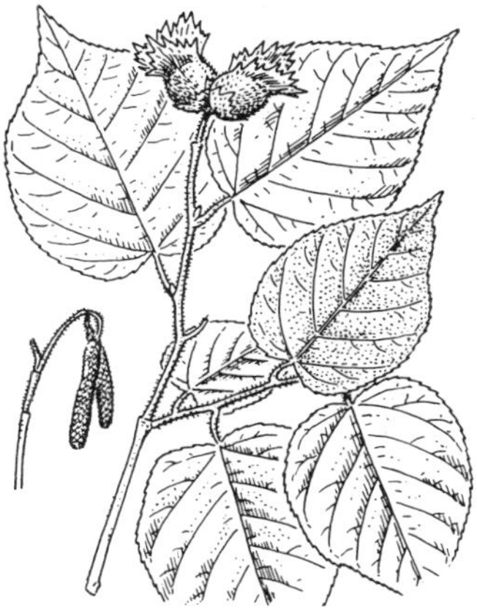

Hazelnuts
Corylus americana

Toasted Hazelnuts

Place a bit of butter in a shallow pan. Add hazelnuts. Sprinkle with salt. Bake 30 minutes at 300 degrees. Try with sugar and cinnamon.

Nougat

- 2 cups sugar
- 1/2 cup corn syrup
- 1 cup water
- 4 egg whites
- 1 teaspoon vanilla
- 1 1/2 cuts nut meats
- 1/2 cup candied cherries

Combine half the water, sugar and corn syrup. Boil to stiff ball stage (246 degrees). Remove from heat and pour slowly over the well beaten egg whites. Continue beating till cool. At the same time, have the other 1/2 of sugar mixture cooking. Cook it to the stiff ball stage and beat into the first mixture. Continue beating till mixture is cool. Add the vanilla, nuts and candied cherry. Spread in prepared pan. Let sit overnight. Cut into pieces and wrap in plastic wrap or waxpaper.

Chestnuts

The Chinese chestnut will soon be a fine foraging food although the great American chestnut seems to be a thing of the past. I have been lucky enough to find these coming up and I still have the stumps decaying. The young trees die before setting nuts. Folks that have the Chinese chestnut trees in their yards are supplying nuts for the squirrels to feed on and plant. However, these nuts seem to be plagued with an insect that lays their eggs in most of the nuts. I find if I gather the nuts and freeze them, I can take care of that without spraying. Pick up the nuts as they fall, wash, place in freezer bags and add water. Freeze them now for your future needs. I don't often use chestnuts as nuts, but more like a vegetable. They can be roasted or boiled for out-of-hand eating. If you are going to roast them, be sure and pierce the shell, because they have a tendency to burst when heated. I have not had this problem with cooking mine by starting with cold water and removing after just 5 minutes, but you should have a lid on the pan to be safe. If I were going to make flour, I would use the chestnut or acorn and save my other nuts for more of the dessert or candy recipes.

Chinese Chestnut
Castanea dentata

Chestnut continued

To prepare, place in a pan, cover with cold water. Bring to a boil and boil for about 5 minutes. Let them cool in the pan of hot water to continue the cooking. Cut them apart, removing each side with the point of a knife. Place in blender with water and chop. Drain the water. I use these in lots of recipes like meat loaf, stews, Jerusalem artichoke salad and, most especially, stuffings.

Chestnut Stuffing

- 1/2 cup chopped celery
- 1/2 cup chopped onion
- 2 cup broth
- 1 tablespoon sage (fresh)
- Cornbread, cubed and dried
- 2 teaspoon salt, if needed
- 1 cup cooked, peeled and ground chestnuts

Saute onion and celery, add chestnuts, broth and seasoning. Add cornbread to make it the consistency you want. Stuff your meat or bake in a pan.

Acorns (Quercus spp.) are not fit to eat as is. They must be hulled, split and have all the bitter leached out. This is done by soaking in water a very long time and changing water often. They will need to be cooked and ground for flour. I only did this once when I was den mother. My den had a wild food supper. Those Cub Scouts are now fathers of Cub Scouts and they didn't forget doing this. But I think it is far too much work for what you get! Give it a try if you'd like. You must mix wheat flour with the acorns to get a palatable bread. Substitute only 1/3 acorn flour in a recipe for best results.

Black walnuts (Juglans nigra) grow in the Northeastern United States. There are other species growing elsewhere and most folks will have access to black walnuts. Scout out the trees for the largest and most easily cracked. Very few folks plant black walnut as nothing much will grow under them. Where the roots spread they will kill most plants, as they produce a poison in the root system. Cows seem to find that lying under a walnut tree in the pasture is a nice place to chew their cud. Being in these locations also makes it easy to harvest these nuts. Black walnuts have a thick green husk that must be removed before drying. The best way I know to remove these is to step on and squash them. With plastic-gloved hands, pick up and loosen any husk left clinging to the nut. The stain is awful and it is most impossible to remove, except to let it wear off. The wood of the black walnut is most beautiful and widely used for fine furniture. The hulls are used for dye, medicine and food. The pickled young immature walnuts will be quite a surprise and the recipe follows.

Black Walnut
Juglans nigra

To dry black walnuts, put them on a porch, in a shed or if you have to, out-of-doors under a tarp. Crack some now and again to see if the nut meat is dry but not brittle. When dry, crack and remove the nut meats. The shells are thick and coarse so cracking is quite a chore. Lots of devices have been designed to help with this but what I find works best is to find a big rock to place them on and then to use a hammer to pound and crack them open.

Once shelled, I then place them in the freezer for year-round use. By doing this, your nuts are at their best. If, however, you leave your walnuts until mid-winter to crack, place them in a dry area. They can still be used. I just think they are better cracked as soon as they are dry.

Never use them before drying as they will have a greenish bitter aftertaste. If not placing the nut meat in a freezer, spread them to dry again. You must be sure they are dry or you will loose all your efforts to mold. After cracking and removing the nut meat, I put the leftover shells out for the birds to finish.

Pickled Black Walnuts

Pickled walnuts are made by picking green immature walnuts. They need to be soft enough to pierce with a large needle. They need to be old enough that the kernel frame is formed. Here in West Virginia that is July. I usually start checking the first of the month until I find it is now time. The time will vary with each year and each area. Pick enough to fill your container. I use a glass 1/2 gallon jar. Each walnut needs to be pierced clear through at least twice. Bring to boil enough vinegar, 2 teaspoons salt, 1 tablespoon pickling spices, a pinch of powdered ginger and a few whole peppercorns. Pour over the walnuts. If you like the taste, add in horseradish, more or less as desired. Put on the lid and forget about it all until next year. I usually shake this now and again throughout the year. When your year is up, remove from the vinegar what you need and slice and serve.

Black Walnut Pie

Beat 3 eggs, add 1/2 cup brown sugar. Melt 1/4 cup butter and add with 1 cup corn syrup. Mix with the egg mixture. Stir in 1 cup finely chopped black walnuts that have been mixed with 1 cup quick cooking rolled oats. Pour into a 9-inch pie shell. Bake at 425 degrees for 10 minutes, then lower heat to 350 degrees and continue baking till crust is nice and browned, about 20 to 25 minutes. You can substitute another cup of chopped walnuts instead of the rolled oats. This will make the walnut flavor much more pronounced.

Black Walnut Salad

This salad is different but you will want it again. Take 3 beets and cook them about half done--crunchy but not yet tender. Grate these with one large sour apple (yellow), 1/2 of a large unpeeled cucumber and 3 dill pickles. Add 1 cup finely sliced celery and 1/2 cup black walnut pieces. Mix 1/2 cup sour cream with 1/2 cup yogurt. Toss all together well and add 1 large sprig of fresh dill chopped. Toss again. Place in refrigerator for several hours and toss now and again to get all the flavor to mingle. Serve on lettuce.

Waldorf Salad

Peel and chop 3 cups apples. If they are pretty and red, you can leave them unpeeled or combine both peeled and unpeeled. Add 1 cup chopped celery and do include the leaves. Now mix in 1/2 cup raisins and 1/2 cup black walnuts. Add boiled salad dressing and let set over night or at least several hours for flavors to mingle and raisins to plump.

Boiled Salad Dressing

In a double boiler, melt 2 tablespoons of butter, beat one egg and add 1 cup sugar and 1 cup vinegar. Mix 1/4 cup flour and 1 teaspoon dry mustard with 1 cup milk. Stir into the pot. Stir all well and cook till thick and bubbly. Cool. Add to the salad, mixing well. You may need to add honey if apples are too sour. This boiled salad dressing is great in potato salad. Mayonnaise can be extended by mixing equal parts of the boiled dressing in the mayonnaise for other salads.

Black Walnut Pudding

Filling

Butter a 9x12 inch baking pan. Combine 2 1/2 cups boiling water, 2 cups brown sugar and 1 tablespoon butter. Stir in 1 cup walnut meats and 1 cup raisins or currants. Put this on to boil while making the batter.

Batter

Cream 1/2 cup shortening with 1 cup sugar. Add vanilla. Sift together 1 3/4 cup flour, 3 teaspoon baking powder and 1/4 teaspoon salt. Stir dry ingredients in the first mixture alternating with 3/4 cup milk. Drop batter by tablespoon full over the syrupy mixture. Bake 350 degrees for 25 to 30 minutes. Serve warm or cold.

Butternut

This nut (Juglans cinerea) is found in some local areas but they are not as plentiful as the black walnut here. Even if they are both walnuts, and can be interchanged in my walnut recipes, there is a distinct difference in flavor. Butternuts grow long rather than round and have a higher fat content. Where the fields at one time had many butternuts now I can hardly find more than one tree. And the squirrels must get their share. What I do find I use in special recipes or eaten from hand. No matter, they are good if not plentiful. I have planted seeds and have small trees, so perhaps some day I'll have plenty. The meat is harder to extract from the shell, but they don't have hulls so you don't have to deal with that. In harvesting, just gather, dry and crack.

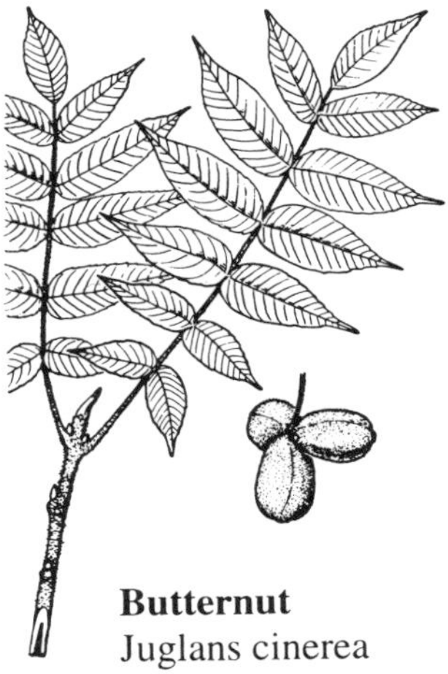

Butternut
Juglans cinerea

Butternut Cake Frosting

Cook 2 cups brown sugar in 1/2 cup water, stirring to dissolve sugar. Boil to 235 degrees on candy thermometer. Beat 2 egg whites stiff. Pour the syrup in a thin stream while continuing to beat the egg whites. Add 1/2 cup of the butternut meats and spread on cake. Cover and let set for several hours to let flavors mingle. Then, enjoy the fruits of your labor. Also, you can use other nuts if you must.

Butternut continued

Candied Butternuts

Combine 1 cup sugar with 1 tablespoon light corn syrup, a sprinkle of salt and 1/2 cup water in a cast iron skillet. Cook and stir till sugar is dissolved. Continue to cook at 238 degrees on candy thermometer. Remove from the heat and add 6 large marshmallows. Stir until melted and creamy. Add 2 1/2 cups of large butternut pieces. Turn onto a lightly buttered platter. Separate pieces to dry. When coating is dry, shake in confectionery sugar.

Butternut Cookies

Mix together 2 cups butter and 1 cup powdered sugar and 1/2 teaspoon salt. Sift together 4 1/4 cups flour and 1 1/2 cups finely chopped butternuts. Mix these all well together and chill over night. Cut dough into small pieces and roll between your hands into balls about the size of a walnut. Bake on ungreased cookie sheet in a 400 degree oven about 10 to 12 minutes. These will not get brown nor should they. While still warm, shake in confectionery sugar. Place on rack to cool. Store in an air-tight container for several days and they will be much better. The longer they stay, the better they are. Black walnuts work equally well.

The Many Other Uses of Plants

Medical plants are many and some have been scientifically proven useful. Some have been proven useless for the claimed treatment. Some plants are also harmful or poison. Some have never been discovered or tested. There is no magic plant or plants. As opposed to the quick action of a pill, plants are usually milder and will take some time to be effective. Here, I am only going to cover the many ways to use some plants, but not the ones to use. Medical uses of plants are a whole different area of study. It will take most of your lifetime and then you will not even be close to covering them all. Also, you need to know what you are doing or you can hurt yourself, as with taking too large doses of yellowroot or comfrey.

Many books can be found on medical uses of plants. The bible of them all seems to be "Back to Eden" by Jethro Kloss. This book was first published in 1939 and has been reprinted many times. It can be ordered from Woodridge Press Publishing Company, P.O. Box 6189, Santa Barbara, California, 93111, or, I'm sure you can get it from most any large book store. It is a must for serious students of the plant world. Rodale Press has several nice books on plants and their uses. The Peterson Field Guides are especially nice: small and easy reference to identifying the different plants.

Dry Salted - If you wish to preserve leaves for winter use, gather, wash, dry well and layer with salt. My Grandmother did this with grape leaves and basil. They are tops this way. Try it. You might like it. Today, I mostly use the freezer.

Liqueur - can be made from many plants and fruits. You can use just one or a combination of plants. It is fun and you might really come up with something you really like. Mash the plant or fruit to a pulp. Place in 1 pint of brandy or white wine. Place in a sunny window to mingle flavors. Strain and bottle. I tried moonshine and rose petals one time. I am going to try sweet woodruff in white wine next. This was called May Wine and much used in Germany.

Bath - These can be aromatic herbs just for nice aroma or they can be plants used for medical reasons. There are two ways to do this. One is to dry the plants, place in a bag and then let your bath water run over it. The other way the plant can be made into a strong tea and added to the bath water. Bath oils can also be made from aromatic plants.

Tisane or Infusion - plant needed and made into a tea and drank regularly as you would take medicine.

Insect Repellent - raw juice rubbed on the skin or made into a strong tea and bathed on the skin. It can also be dried and used as animal bedding or in dresser drawers such as pennyroyal.

Vapors - plant of choice, dried and placed in a vaporizer.

Poultice - strong tea made from plant of choice or leaves placed on an area and kept hot.

Ointments - a salve made with 1 cup bee's wax and 1 cup mineral oil with plant of choice or need. Heat oil and pour over the plant. Let it steep. Strain. Beat this oil infusion and add the bee's wax slowly while continuing to beat. Pour while warm into containers and label. This recipe is for a heavy ointment. If you want it more soft, cut the amount of bee's wax. I use this ointment for callused knees, elbows, etc. Rub on after a hot bath then towel off. I add a bit of borax to my mixture for this.

Tincture - a plant soaked in grain alcohol and used externally only.

Dye - many, many different plants for many different colors and shades of color. The mordant used, the season and growing conditions will also have an effect. This is also a whole other ball game. Lots of folks are today spinning and dyeing fibers. Many good books are available, if that is your thing.

Vinegars - are made by mashing needed plant and pouring over hot vinegar. Let this set in a sunny window two weeks. Strain and bottle. A different dressing can be made by stirring sugar or honey in the hot vinegar before pouring over the plant. Wild rose petals work wonders here. If you only try one vinegar, try this one just once.

Decorative Herbs and Flowers

While you are out there hunting all those edible plants, you will find many useful things for decorating. A pretty fungus, odd shaped branches, stones, flowers and mosses. A pretty what-not can be made from a piece of fungus or stone with moss and / or flowers glued on. Add on a bug or a tiny plastic bird or animal. The chestnut driftwood is just beautiful as are other driftwoods. You will find yourself carrying home some of these pretty things to use for crafts and decorations or gifts.

Most flowers can be dried, but in different ways. Again, this is a whole other ball game and there are lots of books on the subject. If you want to learn more, purchase one or more books. I am most familiar with Phyllis Shaudy's "The Pleasure of Herbs" and "Herbal Treasures," available from Storey Communications, Schoolhouse Road, Pownal, Vermont, 05261. You can't go wrong with either of these.

Potpourri can be made from most flowers. You need the flowers, a fixative and a smelly or oil. A basic recipe contains 4 cups of flowers of a compatible color, 1/2 cup vegetable fiber, at least 1 teaspoon of your scent (essential oil) and 1 tablespoon ground spice like cinnamon, nutmeg, etc. In a glass jar, put the vegetable fiber and pour in the oil and spice. Shake and let this set a few days for all to mingle. Then add the dried flowers. Make sure they are completely dry or they will mold. Usually a white flower and a bit of greenery is added to the flowers. Whole spices can be used instead of powdered. You can make sachets for drawers, closets, clothes boxes, suitcases and gifts from this.

Pressed flowers are made by gathering the flowers and placing them in a heavy book to press and use further. After drying, make pictures, placements and / cards. Try Queen Anne's Lace this way and you can make a beautiful Victorian Christmas tree for your next holidays. Make a nylon hanger and spray, then sprinkle on diamond dust.

Wreaths

Many things can be found to make wreaths. All kinds of vines from greenbrier to grape.

Woodruff wreaths - The wreaths I like the most are made from sweet woodruff. Gather the longest you can find the night before use, so it will lose some moisture. Make a wreath form from heavy wire from 4 inches to 16 inches. Gather the woodruff by the handful and start wrapping this around the wire. Go in one direction and continue till wire is covered completely. Add a bit of babies breath, a sprig of dried flowers and a bow. Hang to dry and enjoy the aroma a year or more.

Solid woodruff wreaths are made by the same method except they must be full and tightly wound with nylon or fishing cord then dried. Choose the color you want and go gather your flowers and dry. A nice combinations is Black-eyed Susans, goldenrod and fern. After the woodruff wreath is dry, get out a glue gun and go to work. Glue flowers on the inside of the wreath first, then the outside edge. Finally glue flowers to the top, then glue in a few green leaves or fern to hide

any bare spots. Make a hanger from the fishing line or nylon thread. Add a pretty bow and your wreath is done. It can be sprayed with hair spray to set everything.

Pine cone wreaths are both beautiful as well as long-lasting. A form for these can be found at most craft stores. The first of everything is always the hardest but practice will make perfect and you can make all your Christmas gifts from nature. The pine cones need to be baked 200 degrees till all have opened. This will get ride of any bugs inside and melting of the sap will make them shiny like they have been sprayed with varnish.

The many uses of the wild plants are bound only by your imagination.

Wild Mushrooms

These are wonderful and abundant foods that grow in both fields and woods, and, they can be gathered year-round. I have listed only three here. They are the three I know. Absolutely never pick and consume a wild mushroom if you don't know it well. Some are as deadly as they are delicious. Some good ones look nearly like a poison one. Sometimes an experienced forager will pick the look-alike. The best way to learn the mushrooms is go picking with the old pro.

Morels (Morchella spp.)

These are plentiful and come up in the early spring. After a long winter of being indoors and before garden time my body and soul needs a good hike. Most folk's morel patch is a well kept secret. They are probably the best of the wild mushrooms. I think each to its own time is the best. I try to gather a peck basket full and I dry most of these for year- round use. When finding your morels, grasp and pull from the ground, cut off the attached dirt and roots, leave this in the woods and brush off any clinging leaves or dirt. A soft brush is good for this. When drying, one must not wash these mushrooms. I slice them in half and lay them on a cloth-lined screen to dry.

Sometimes you will find bugs inside the older mature ones. These I soak in salt water, saute in butter and eat for supper or place in the refrigerator for later. Never pick all these or any other wild foods. Leave some for the animals and Mother Nature. I try not to pick a mushroom that is too old and mature. You usually can tell as they are larger, darker and seem wilted. The little bugs I find in them look like woodland fleas. However careful I am, I will always have a few with bugs. Over the years, I have always poured my cleaning water out in the same one wooded spot below my house. I now have a patch of mushrooms very close by. For eating fresh, I just swish my bugless mushrooms in cold water, drain, dust with flour and saute in butter and sprinkle with a bit of salt and pepper. Plenty of these are prepared and served in the place of meat. The dried ones I wash and then put in boiling water to plump, then use anywhere I want mushrooms. Sauteed with a steak, or stuffing; but, most especially, I like them in soup. On a cold winter day, a bowl of cream of mushroom soup is tops.

Wild Mushroom Soup

Put 1/4 cup dry morels in 1 cup boiling water. Add 2 cups chicken stock, cream and a cornstarch thickening. Salt, pepper and butter to taste.

I have identified 4 different species of these morels. Some of them never get much over one or one-half inch tall and are thicker. These are the ones I like to dry. They are known as Morchella esculenta. Then there is one called Morchella elata. It is tall with more stem then top. These are also nice for breading. Don't discard the stem as I've seen some do. It's as good as the top. There is also no need to soak these over night in salt water. These seem to be more prone to the little bugs, but why ruin all your mushrooms just to drown a few fleas. If you find one with bugs, plant it to grow more by just tossing to the ground. As far as I know, no morel is poisonous if cooked, but don't eat them raw. They are easy to identify and only grow in certain areas, so once found you can return again and again. If you treat the fungi with respect, the turkey doesn't scratch up the area and if it rains enough, that area will produce all the morels you need. There are several different species including the black_(Morchella deliciosa) and giant (Morchella crassipes). They mostly all look alike in structure but the spongy parts look different. They can be used interchangeable in any recipe. There are several other species of morels but this is what I have near me. If you have different ones, learn about each before sampling.

Puffball (Calvatia gigantea)
This is a nice find in the summer after a nice rain and in the hay meadows. They are not as dependable in returning, but if you see a white spot in the grass that wasn't there yesterday check it out now. They grow huge, baseball size or bigger. Put your hand under, lift up and slice off the roots. Cut open and if you have got there soon enough, it will look like whipped white cream cheese. If it has any streaks of brown or brown juice, leave it there as it is not good and probably they are all bad, so better luck next time. Use these as a favorite in soup or just saute them now. They will not keep in the refrigerator and they also won't dry. So, when you find 'em, you eat 'em. There are many species of these, but I use just this one.

Button Mushrooms (Argaricus bisporus) are the wild cousins of the commercial mushrooms. They have close look-alikes but a little studying will soon teach you the difference. The easiest way is to check the under side. They are a pretty soft pink and as they age they turn brownish to blackish. They are also easy to grow and kits are available. They seldom come up in the same place. Use them in any way you would the commercial ones.

Perhaps someday I will learn more of the edible mushrooms, but I now have an ample year-round supply. I can feel safe and enjoy what I have. I hope you will learn these and enjoy them too.

Wild Honey, Honey Bees and Bee's Wax

Wild honey has been gathered for ages and you can still find a bee tree if you set about trying. But then to get the honey you have to destroy the tree and will probably destroy the bees. I don't think we have a bee to lose, let alone a whole hive. We do tend to take them for granted and we really shouldn't. If you can, it's best to keep a few hives of bees for your own use. I keep one hive and that's enough for the average family. If this is not possible, I bet there is someone nearby who keeps bees and will be your supplier. Your own wild bees will keep things pollinated and give you plenty of honey for all kinds of things. I use lots of bee products. First, I like honey; second, I seem to have an intolerance to sugar; and last, it is so versatile.

Research is being done on bee products in the treatment of allergies. It is thought that honey and honeycomb made from local flowers will help the immune system to prevent allergies and the bee venom for arthritis. Only time and research will prove if these theories are true. Then there is bee pollen and royal jelly with all its claims.

If the occasion arises and a tree must be destroyed, you can harvest the honey and not all will be lost.

Gather the honey in a metal container. Set this container down in a larger container of water and heat slowly, just enough to melt the wax. The wax will all float to the top as it melts. Let the containers of honey-water cool overnight. In the morning, pry off the chunk of solid wax. Slip 2 dowel sticks under the wax and let the clinging honey drip off all day. This is not a hurry-up kind of job, but soon you will have your honey. Impurities are in the solid mass of wax. Wash off any clinging honey and put chunk of wax aside to dry. Reheat the honey container just enough so the honey will flow easily. Pour honey into sterilized jars, cool and tighten down the lids. If your honey gets sugary before using, remove the jar lid and place the jar in a pan of hot, but not boiling, water. It will return to liquid. The type of vegetation the bees are visiting determines this, although most all flower honey will sooner or later turn to sugar. If stored in a cold place, it will sugar sooner. As for the cans and other equipment I use, I have a special set. Because bee's wax is darn near impossible to remove from anything, I never use these items for anything else and I store it all away in paper bags between uses.

Now, to the bee's wax. It must be cleaned. It must be melted in a double boiler. This is absolutely necessary and never leave it on the heat unattended. Break the wax and place in a muslin bag and add a rock or so to keep the bag from floating. Place this in the top of the double boiler with water to cover several inches. I usually do my wax in a recycled 3 pound coffee can which, at I noted above, I use for nothing else. Sit this container in the larger one and place on the heat. Let this heat and the wax will flow to the top while the impurities stay in the muslin and rock bag. Remove from heat and let set till tomorrow. Remove the nice round of pure, clean wax and toss the rest. This wax can be used for candles, waxing things like thread, zippers, squeaky doors, boots, etc. I will melt my cleaned wax enough to pour into molds to sell. I use recycled paper drinking cups and orange juice cans. Just peel off the paper and it's ready to go.

Honey Glaze

Place 2 tablespoons of butter in skillet. Melt and stir in 1/2 cup honey. Stir and heat to boiling. Remove and pour on item to be glazed.

Honey Butter

1 cup honey
1 cup real butter

Leave the ingredients at room temperature overnight. Mix all well. Place in the refrigerator and keep cold or it will separate. You may add a spice of your choice if you like. I sometimes use cinnamon. Use in place of butter on toast, etc. It's yummy!

Country Lemonade

2 cups honey
1 cup good homemade vinegar
1 tablespoon or more of (commercial) ginger

Heat vinegar and pour over the ginger root . When cool, stir in the honey. Strain out the roots. Store in refrigerator till used. Add about 3 tablespoons to a glass of water and ice cubes. Stir.
NOTE: Wild ginger is difficult to find now and, in fact, is endangered due to over-gathering. Use only commercial ginger.

Honeyed Popcorn

This is usually kept on hand in the winter. It is not only a good snack but the price is right. I keep a special good-grade plastic bucket with lid to store this in. Popcorn balls can also be formed from this syrup. Pop 3/4 cup popcorn or whatever amount you need to get a gallon of popped corn.

1. Set the oven on 300 degrees.
2. Lightly butter a large bowl or pan and 2 large baking pans.
3. Place 1/2 cup butter in cast iron skillet, melt and add 1/2 cup honey. Heat to boiling while corn is popping. You can make more if you like, just use equal parts of real butter and honey.
4. As corn pops, empty into large bowl or pan.
5. When all corn is popped, add the honey syrup. Mix well or make popcorn balls.
6. Place loose popcorn on the large baking pans and place in oven to dry.
7. Remove from oven and use or store in a tightly closed container.

Photo by Mike Furbee

Wild Game Animals

NOTES

Large Wild Game Animals

Any of the large game animals (deer, elk, moose, antelope, bear) are a challenge and quite a bit of work, if butchered and prepared properly. It will go a long way toward extending the food budget and the meat is every bit as good as beef, if prepared properly. The kill should be quick, preferably with one shot, leg scent removed, bled immediately, gutted (saving the liver and heart) and hung. Skin animal being sure not to let the hairy side of the skin touch the meat, as it will give a bad flavor. Let the carcass hang a few days, in a cold place for the meat to cure. Remove all fat that you can when dressing the animal. When the meat is cool, remove remaining fat. Most of the strong flavor will be in the fat.

When cutting up the carcass you will have the same cuts of meat as a beef will have. They will be smaller with little fat or cholesterol. If you have no problem with cholesterol you can add fat when preparing your meat. Any way you fix a corresponding piece of beef will work with this game except you can add the fat. There is a lot of controversy about soaking in water with added salt, vinegar or soda. The only pieces I soak are where the animal was shot and organ meats. Would you take a prime piece of beef and soak it in any solution? If you doubt me, try it sometime and see how good that beef is. If your animal has been killed quickly, dressed and prepared properly it will be good. An animal that has been chased by dogs and/or shot to pieces, hauled around or left till later to dress, will not taste like one done properly. Remember that animal gave all it had, its life for you. Utilize it properly and use it all. Mostly, I use deer because that is what I have. However, these recipes work just as well for the others.

Large Wild Game Animals continued

I have only been able to find two bear but they were as different as day and night. One was tough and gamey while the other was tender and tasty. With all these recipes for meat, a lot of the cook's success depends on the age, killing, butchering and aging of the meat. Cool the carcass till almost frozen so the fat can be removed and the meat cut up. Bear fat is fine for preserving leather, soap, ointment and lotions. Boil the fat in water and skim off for further use. Bear is a little more gamey than the other large game, in my opinion. The flavor comes from any fat you could not remove.

As the cook, the first thing you will have to deal with are the organ meats--kidney, brains, liver and heart. Place in the refrigerator. When ready to prepare, place the liver in the freezer unwrapped, you want to just harden it to make slicing easier. Heart--cut off the fat and arteries at the top. Split and wipe out the blood. Freeze for future use. See recipes in sections below for using each of these meats.

Regarding the brining/corning of wild meats, this method of preservation is not for the novice and it is not recommended by the U.S. Department of Agriculture. I know some folks still use it, but today it really should not be done. It is a long drawn-out process and you can lose all your meat or make yourself very sick. Brining is an old nearly forgotten process. We really don't need to do it today what with all our refrigeration. I always made corned meat as I happen to like it very much. A supper of corned meat, potatoes, turnip and cabbage all slowly cooked together and served up with corn bread just can't be beat. If you want to try brining meat, be safe and buy a bag of Morton's Tender-Quick and follow directions.

Really gamey-tasting meat can be carbonated:

Carbonate Wild Meat

(for gamey meat)

One 3-5 pound roast
Peanut oil
Salt-pepper, rubbed in the meat
8 large onions quartered
1 can ginger ale or beer

Sear the meat on all sides in the peanut oil. Lower the heat to a low simmer. Add the onions that have been cut into quarters. Add the carbonated liquid. Cover and cook slowly several hours. Mushroom soup may be added when finished cooking. If I have wild mushrooms, I add them.

Wild Game Sausage

5 pounds ground meat
2 1/2 pounds ground pork fat
1/2 cup brown sugar
4 tablespoons salt (Kosher)
1 tablespoon black pepper
1 teaspoon dry sage
1/8 teaspoon dried ground garlic
1/4 teaspoon dried thyme
1/4 teaspoon red pepper, crushed--more spices, if you like

Grind your meats and let set at room temperature. Mix in all the spices with your hands somewhat like you do bread. Pull the bottom part up and push down. Do this every 3-4 hours all day long. Every bit of the spices must be worked all through the meat. Let it set overnight in a cool place for the flavors to mingle. No, it won't spoil. Now, for final preparation, if you make into patties and freeze, it must be double wrapped. It also must be used in 3-4 months. You can also can it, using any meat canning recipe.

Wild Game Crumble Sausage Gravy

Crumble the amount of sausage you will need into a black iron skillet and fry. Stir in 1/4 cup flour and brown. Stir all the while. Now add water, milk or a combination of the two. Adjust seasoning, maybe a little more salt or pepper. Serve this over hot biscuits.

Wild Game Meat Loaf

Take 2 pounds ground meat, add 1 cup chopped tomatoes, 1 tablespoon salt and pepper and 1/2 cup of each of the following: grated carrots, chopped onion and celery, boiled and mashed chestnuts. These should all be sauted till tender. Add to the meat and mix. Add 1-2 eggs, a dash of Worcestershire sauce and enough bread crumbs to have a nice firm loaf. You can pour on most any kind of fat to make it more like regular meatloaf, if you want. However, the vegetables help take care of this. Place in a loaf pan. Bake uncovered at 350 degrees for 1 hours.

Wild Game Roasts--Baked or Boiled

1-2 pound pieces of roast	4 small onions
4 sticks of celery	4 potatoes
4 carrots	Herbs of choice

Have a black iron skillet hot with fat. Sear the meat on both sides. Leave in the skillet for boiling but place in roasting pan for roasting. Pour over this, 4 cups of water, broth or tomato juice or any combination. Cover and cook slowly for 1 hour. A bay leaf, salt and pepper should be added before cooking. You can add the herbs to your own liking. I sometimes use thyme and garlic. Red wine may be used as part of the liquid. By varying the cooking and seasoning, you will not become bored using all your meat. Add vegetables and continue cooking till tender.

Wild Game Meat and Chili Beans

1 pound cooked pinto or kidney beans
2 pounds ground meat
1 large onion, chopped fine
Hot sauce to your taste
Chili powder to your taste
2 cloves of garlic, mashed
1 tablespoon salt
Tomato Juice

Place all in stock pot. Add water to cover. Bring to a boil. Keep adding tomato juice to keep the beans covered. Cook slowly several hours until beans are bursting. Add chili the last half hour of cooking.

West Virginia Wild Game Hot Dog Sauce

1 pint water
1 cup onions
1 large garlic clove
1 1/2 teaspoon dry mustard
2 tablespoons chili powder
1 pound ground meat
1/2 cup celery
1 can tomato paste
Salt to taste
1 tablespoon honey
1 teaspoon each of paprika, nutmeg, ginger
1/2 teaspoon each allspice, cloves, cinnamon
1 tablespoon each cocoa, vinegar, pepper
1/4 cup flour mixed with 1/2 cup water

Into a large heavy pot, put the water to heat. Crumble in the ground meat and break up well with a fork. Grind the vegetables and place in the pot. Cook till tender. Add more water as necessary to just cover the pot ingredients. Add the tomato paste and stir to dissolve. Add spices. Bring to boiling and add the flour and water, that has been made into a paste. Simmer several hours.

Wild Game Meat Balls

1 pound ground meat
1/4 cup fresh parsley chopped
1/4 cup Parmesan cheese grated
Milk to soften the bread crumbs
1-2 cups dry bread crumbs
1 beaten egg
1 teaspoon salt

Mix all together and make the meat balls. Brown on all sides.
Sauce--1cup chopped onion and 1 or more cloves of garlic mashed. Cook these till limp and add to the meatball pot. Cover with 4 cups tomato juice. Add a bay leaf and sprinke on 1/4 teaspoon allspice, 1 tablespoon fresh oregano and 1 tablespoon fresh basil. If using dry herbs, use less, about 1 teaspoon of basil and oregano. Add a few pieces of chicken parts, like the backs and neck. These are used for flavor only. Remove the chicken bones and bay leaf before serving. Cook your sauce long and on very low heat till thick. I use my canned tomato juice. You can use tomato paste and water, if you prefer.

Scrapple

Here is another old and requested recipe often used fried as a breakfast food.

2 cups ground pork
3 cups meat broth
1 teaspoon black pepper
3 dashes hot sauce
2 cups ground red meat
3 teaspoons salt
2 tablespoon sage or thyme
1 cup cornmeal

Combine meats and broth and bring to a boil. The pork should have a bit of fat in it. Sprinkle in the corn meal while stirring. Lower heat and cook slowly about 30 minutes. Stir in the spices a few minutes before removing from the fire. Mold into a good serving size by pouring this into a recycled tin cans or anything that makes a nice serving size. It will firm up. Slice off your scrapple in the width you like and fry.

Wild Game Mincemeat

I use any kind of wild red meat I have on hand, about 4 pounds cooked tender in salt water. Chop the meat fine, add to the pot. Reserve the meat broth for something else. I do not use suet or fat for my mincemeat--it can be added if you like. Into a large crock pot place these ingredients in the order given:

2 quarts cider	2 cups brown sugar
3 cups peeled and chopped apples	3 cup honey

1 tablespoon each of cinnamon, ginger and allspice
6 cups various wild dried fruit--peaches, berries, cherries, currents, apples, etc.
Brandy

Add the cooked, chopped meat. Cover the crock pot and cook on low heat about 6 hours. Check and stir up the fruits, from the bottom, making sure all fruit is done. Turn off the crock pot so the mincemeat is lukewarm but not cold. Stir in 1 cup of good brandy. Cover the crock pot and let it set till morning. It will keep for several days this way or it can be made in pies, cookies, etc. I have never canned this but if any is left over, it can be frozen. I usually make this at hunting time that comes around the Winter holidays. I make it up into gifts, so I seldom have any left.

Wild Game Vegetable Soup

Day 1--Cook until the meat falls from the bone a large group of bones with some meat clinging. Place these in a large, 12 quart, stock pot. Add 1 gallon water and 1 tablespoon salt.

Day 2--Remove what meat is on the bones and discard bones. You may want to fry a pound of gound meat to add to this if a more meaty soup is wanted. Just crumble the ground meat in a hot oiled and salted fry pan. Add all this to the pot. Heat the broth and add the following vegetables:

4 cups diced potatoes
1 cup each of the following chopped: celery, onions, carrots, turnips, cabbage

Let these cook several hours slowly. When they are tender, add 1 cup each of while kernel corn, peas and green beans. Let these cook 1 hour more, slowly. The longer and slower it cooks the better, and it's always better the next day. This makes a large quantity of soup which can be frozen for later use. If the liquid evaporates, add more broth or tomato juice. I sometimes add dry beans that have been soaked overnight to the first vegetable list. I also sometimes leave out the potatoes and use 1 cup dry barley. The potatoes do not freeze well but usually I use what I have on hand. Very often I make a much smaller batch and use mostly leftovers. However you make vegetable soup, it's good. If you are making this for freezing, substitute rice or barley for the potatoes.

Corned Meat Stew

2 cups chopped corn meat	2 chopped onions
6 chopped potatoes	4 cups tomatoes
1 tablespoon sugar	1 cup peas

In an electric skillet place everything except the tomatoes and peas. Put on water to cover the vegetables and cook till tender. Cook slowly on simmer. When tender add the tomatoes and peas. Cook till done. Any leftovers are always better the next day.

Red Flannel Hash

1 cup cooked and chopped beets
3 cups cooked and chopped potatoes
2 cups cooked and chopped corned bear
1 large onion chopped
1/4 cup whole milk or cream

Combine all except milk and fry in cast iron skillet with ham fat. Stir or turn when done, add the milk and sprinkle on pepper. Serve.

Corned Meat and Cabbage

3 cups corned meat or piece that size, water to cover. Bring to a boil and cook till tender. Add 6 whole potatoes. Cover and cook till done. Add 1 head of cabbage that has been cut into wedges. Cook till cabbage is tender. Serve. Corn bread and buttermilk was usually served with this.

Wild Game Summer Sausage

5 pounds ground wild meat
3 tbsp. coarse ground black pepper
1 tbsp. dried & powdered wild garlic
1 tablespoon mustard seed
1 teaspoon Liquid Smoke
1 teaspoon or more hot sauce

Mix all together and continue as for sausage. Roll out in a 3-inch wide roll. Place on rack in oven and bake at 175 degrees for 8 hours or until firm and dry.

Wild Game Pizza

In a warm bowl, add 1/2 cup warm water, 1 tablespoon yeast, a pinch of sugar, 1 teaspoon salt and 1/2 cup unbleached flour. Stir all and set in a warm place to rise. About 30 minutes should be enough. Now, stir in 1 tablespoon olive oil and enough flour to make a soft dough. You will need about 2 cups of flour for the entire thing and having enough for rolling. Prepare a cookie sheet by brushing with oil and dusting with corn meal. Let the dough rise 20 minutes before rolling. This dough is very elastic and will need to be patted, pulled and stretched to get it to cover the pan. Let the dough set like this to rise till you get your topping finished. You will need about 2 cups of tomato sauce. It can be any leftover spaghetti sauce, Mom's Chili Sauce or even just plain tomatoes, mashed. Thinly sliced or grated mozzarella cheese, sausage fried, summer sausage, pepperoni, or leftover meat balls. You can add most anything you want--peppers, mushrooms, sauted onions or all of these. Brush oil on the dough and cover with the tomato sauce. Sprinkle with 1 tablespoon oregano and hot sauce, if you like. Now add the cheese and other fillings. If you have any tomato sauce left, drizzle it on top. Bake at 350 degrees for about 40 minutes, till the filling is all bubbly and the crust is brown. Remove from oven. The easiest way to cut this is with your kitchen scissors.

Wild Game Jerky

Jerky is made from tough undesirable cuts of the meat especially the belly. Always cut your meat with the grain. Just the opposite for other cuts. It is a fine nibble food. I marinate my meat, that has been cut in strips no wider than 1 inch. Add Worchestershire sauce, salt and a sprinkle of dry garlic if you like garlic. Let it set to marinate 24 hours, stirring now and again. Place in warm oven, no hotter than 200 degrees till dry and bendable, but not to a crisp. I start it on a foil-lined cookie sheet till most of the marinade is absorbed. Then I lay it directly on the oven rack. This helps when it comes time to clean the oven and for no other reason. I then place it in a recycled cardboard oats box, uncovered, on the top of the refrigerator, to make sure it is completely dry. I rarely get around to storing it in a closed container before it is consumed.

Wild Game Pepperoni

5 pounds ground meat
3 tablespoons Morton Tender-Quick
1/4 teaspoon dry powdered wild garlic
1 tablespoon crushed fennel seed
1 tablespoon Liquid Smoke
1 tablespoon Kosher salt
1 tablespoon hot sauce or to your liking

Mix all together and do the same as you would for sausage. Roll out in stick form and bake in a very slow oven (about the lowest setting, 150 degrees) for about 8 hours. Cut a piece in the center of the stick making sure it is finished.

Pepperoni Rolls Dough

Since my hometown is the place where Pepperoni Rolls were invented, I will include a bit about them here. It seems the coal miners of long ago took homemade rolls and a stick of pepperoni in lunch boxes to the mines. Someone came up with the idea of baking the pepperoni inside the rolls. The first bakery, we know of, that started baking these for sale was Country Club Bakery in 1929 at Fairmont, West Virginia. This State is still the only one mass producing pepperoni rolls and distributing them in Eastern states

1 package dry yeast   1 1/4 cups warm water to dissolve yeast
1 teaspoon sugar

Mix and stir. Let this set 30 minutes. Add 1/4 cup oil and stir in 4 cups of white flour. Knead. Set in a warm place to rise until double in bulk. Keep out of any draft and don't let it get cold. Cut the pepperoni into 3-inch length wise strips. When the dough has risen, work down and cut into 12 equal pieces. Flatten each section and fold in the pepperoni strips, 2-4 each should do it. Let them set and rise in any bread pan, but a cookie sheet works best. Preheat oven to 375 degrees and bake 30 minutes. They are now ready to eat or go to a picnic. Very often they are heated, like a hot dog bun, sliced open and hot dog sauce is added.

Wild Game Neck and Backbone

These are all slowly boiled with a bit of vinegar till tender. The vinegar is used to extract all the calcium from the bones. Some folks cook these bones twice but I don't. My bones are fed to the dogs or burned in my wood burner producing bone meal for my garden. You see nothing needs to be wasted. The meat is picked from the bones and together with the stock it is canned. I use the meat for barbecues, mincemeat and the stock for gravy and soup. See section on Woodchuck for barbecue recipe or use a bottled one of your choice.

Meat Stock

After you have finished butchering your animal, you are left with all those meatless bones. They can be utilized by baking until very brown then cooking a very long time in water. Remove the bones and strain out the fat. Return to boil some more till reduced at least in half or less. Seasoning can be added such as salt, pepper, onion celery tops and a tiny bit of garlic, if you like. I strain again and either can this stock (following meat instructions from your pressure canner) or it can be frozen. It's nice for gravies or soups, but lots of work.

Natural Gelatin

Really want to be authentic with everything? You can make gelatin by cooking bones, any bones, then draining and boiling the remaining broth until thick. Chill the broth and adjust to the desired gel thickness you want by adding water. Different kinds of bones make different thickness of gel. The trick is that you can never tell the thickness level until it cools and sets. If what you get is too thick, add a bit of water, reheat and let set again. It will re-gel. Keep doing this until you get the thickness of gel you want.

Other Wild Game Tough Cuts of Meats

Make slits in the meats and tuck in slivers of garlic. Rub all over the meat with salt and pepper. Let set 1 hour for flavor to be absorbed. Sear meat on both sides in hot skillet. Place in pot and cover with strong coffee. Cook covered very slowly till tender. Bring to boil and add the tough dumplings and boil covered 20 minutes.

Dad's Tough Dumplings

1 egg beaten	1 cup of fresh bread crumbs
1 cup flour	Water for firm ball

Work this all together. If egg is small you may need a little water. Form a ball. Wrap in plastic wrap and let sit to rest. Grate this dough ball on to a wet plate. Use large side of grater. You can roll out ald cut into stripes, if you prefer. slide into boiling broth of any kind. My Dad liked this with ham cooked with dry beans.

The Organ Meats

Stuffed Wild Game Heart

Cook in salted water and herbs of your choice such as bay, sage or hot peppers. When tender, cover and stuff with a stuffing. Add unpeeled sweet potatoes and bake at 350 degrees until the potatoes are tender. Make a good rich gravy from the pan liquid that you cooked the heart in. Serve with another vegetable, salad and wild grape ketchup. The heart can also be ground with your hamburger, sausage and made into jerky.

Wild Game Liver

Hopefully, by now the liver has ice crystals in it and not frozen solid. The slices should be all the same thickness of thin. If the liver is too slippery, flour it and your hands lightly to help when slicing. More liver is ruined by overcooking than any other food. I have tried several different coatings, but buckwheat flour is my choice. Cook over high heat a few minutes on each side. Serve your fried liver with onions that are prepared in another skillet and mixed when the liver is prepared. If your children think they don't like liver, try french frying it like potatoes. If a liver is near or in the shot area, I use it by boiling, grinding and making a liver loaf.

Wild Game Liver Loaf

1 pound boiled liver
1/2 pound pork sausage
2 cups bread crumbs
1 chopped onion
1 tablespoon salt
2 beaten eggs
Broth to moisten bread

Grind the boiled liver. Mix in the other ingredients. Add enough broth to moisten. Shape into a loaf. Press into a 9x5x3 loaf pan. Bake at 350 degrees for 1 hour.

Wild Game Liver with Rice and Tomato

1 pound liver (cubed, floured and sauted)
1 cup rice (prepared according to box directions)
Heat 2 cups salsa or Mom's Chili sauce
1/2 pound bacon, fried crisp

Prepare all separately. Place rice on serving plate, then the liver bits. Pour the salsa over these then sprinkle on the crumbled bacon. Serve.

Mom's Chili Sauce

This is an old family recipe. It can be canned for winter use.

1 peck very ripe tomatoes, peeled and chopped
4 large onions, chopped   4 large green peppers
1 to 2 red hot peppers   1 cup vinegar
1/2 to 1 cup honey (depending sourness of tomatoes)
1 tablespoon salt   1 tablespoon sugar
1 tablespoon mustard seed   1 tablespoon pepper
2 tablespoons pickling spices

Tie spices in a muslin bag and remove before placing in jars. Mix all together and cook till done. Place in sterilized jar and process in hot water bath for 20 minutes.

Wild Game Kidneys

My English Grandmother made a kidney pie and also blood pudding, neither of these have I tried. Kidneys need to have the skin and all membranes removed. A small pair of scissors work best to accomplish this chore. Wash. Cut in half to help remove the tubes. Place in a pan of water to soak over night. I usually put in 1 tablespoon wine vinegar especially if it is from an old animal. When cooked, cool and thinly slice, dust with flour. Saute in bacon fat. Don't overcook. Remove meat from skillet (black iron is best), pour in 1/2 cup beer to deglaze pan. Pour this over the sauted kidney. Serve over rice. They can be added to an omelet for breakfast eating. Here add a little bacon to the skillet when frying. Remove and crumble before adding to the omelet.

Wild Game Brains

Wash the brains in cold water to help remove the membranes. Check for bone fragments. Place in salt water and cook just briefly to firm and finish removing membrane. Cool. Place chopped brains in bowl with 6 beaten eggs, salt and pepper. Scramble in bacon fat. This dish is traditionally served at breakfast.

Wild Game Tongue

Scrape and scrub well in vinegar water. Place in water and cook till tender. This will take an hour or more depending on the age of the animal. Bay leaf, marjoram or thyme, onion and salt can be added to the cooking water. Cool and peel the tongue. It can be served sliced thinly, either warm or cold. I usually add this to the liver loaf or sausage. Serve cold with a horseradish sauce, grape ketchup or mustard. To serve hot, use 2 cups of the cooking broth and make gravy. Add the thinly sliced tongue. Nice with mashed potatoes and biscuits.

Curing Meat with Smoke - Salt

This is an age old art and I had intended to omit the process, but it is one about which most questions are asked. I do not recommend the process but prefer the newer method using the Morton Tender-Quick. The Department of Agriculture does not recommend this process either. It is not for the novice. You can get sick from food poisoning or lose all your meat if every step is not correct. The Morton Salt Company has a number of products you can buy for home curing of meats. They have a dry cure with or without smoke and a wet cure mix both with which you will be safe and the end product will be better. I suggest you start with one of these, then, if you must, work up to doing it with salt and smoke. In days gone by, our forebearers had only salt, smoke and the sun for drying. That's not the case today.

For all those who ask, however, here's how. First, we must make the distinction of what brining/corning and pickling meat is. This process is called pickling by some. Brining/corning is with salt and pickling is done with vinegar. So, it's correct when it's called brining as no one wants a sour meat. Save the pickling way of preserving for vegetables. Brining is the same as corning, as in corned beef.

Dry Curing--Start with a clean wooded surface. Watch out for the wood you use as you don't want your meat to taste like pine or some other woods. Poplar or oak is fine. Spread on 1 or more inches of salt, lay down the meat and cover with more salt. Turn and do this till meat has retained all the salt it can and is dry. Never use any iodine salt and keep metal from touching any part of the meat. Proceed with the smoking.

Water or Wet Brining/Corning--First you will have to find a non-metal container. In days gone by, that was a wooden barrel or 20 gallon crock. They are not available today, so we'll have to use plastic. Make sure your plastic is of good grade. Some of these plastics are harmful to your health. Next, you will need to make a salt solution that will float a raw uncracked egg. Dissolve 4 cups salt in 4 quarts of warm water. I put 1 cup of salt in 3/4 quart of water and shake to dissolve. Let the solution cool. Fill dissolved salt jars full of water. Pour all into a container. Drop in the egg now, add cold water till the egg begins to sink but is still bobbing on top of the salt water, breaking the water surface. Remove egg from the solution and place the meat in it. Make sure all the meat is under the solution all the time. A plate with a quart jar of water will hold it under. Turn the pieces of meat for 7 days, remove from brine, and hang to dry for smoking. It can be smoked now--a fire built and smoked every day for a week. Use green hickory, apple and corn cobs. The final day, add a bit of sassafras wood. So, now you have ham. It's an awful lot of work but, oh, so good! Other woods can be used but stay away from pines and preserved woods. The nuts and fruit woods, except cherry and peach, seem to be the best. However, some folks swear by just maple or corncob.

Smoking--There are two methods of smoking, cool and hot. I use the cool way--very little smoke and no heat. With the hot smoke you can cook your meat in a hurry. A little smoke over a long period of time, with just hanging days between is best. It lets the smoke enter the meat slowly. Meat must be kept cool but don't allow it to freeze between smokings.

The Smoke House-- I have read about 55 gallon barrels, old refrigerators and various other ways to build a smokehouse. I tried the 55 gallon barrel arrangement but it's the pits. Every time I got ready or needed to smoke, it rained, sleeted, hailed or the wind blew. My opinion is, if you are going to all that work, prepare first. You need a 4x4 building on a rock or block foundation, well built, cracks covered and a good solid locking door. There should be enough air spaces around the door so the fire will have enough air to burn. The floor should be dirt with an indentation in the center, about a foot wide and a foot deep. Hang the meat with S-shaped hooks with space between so the smoke can get around the meat. Build the fire each morning and add corn cobs to keep it going. Remember a little smoke will go a long way and the meat needs to dry too. When you have finished with the smoking, let the meat hang a few days before using.

Small Wild Game

Rabbits were available every Fall and hunted for food on the table before hog butchering time. Both my parents and I raised rabbits for use year-round. I know in the city and suburban area, rabbits are a pest and hated. Here on the farm it is different and they have plenty of food without eating my garden. There is always rock and brush piles to live in, so I have no problem. They are all white meat, little or few calories, no cholesterol and can be fixed in many ways. A young rabbit needs to be cooked this way:

Braised Rabbit

Clean and cut up the rabbit. Pat dry and sprinkle with salt, pepper. You can use a smidgen of powdered garlic or onion if you like. Dust with flour. Have ready a hot iron skillet with a bit of fat in it. I use chicken fat or olive oil. Brown on both sides and lower heat. Cook slowly until tender. You can add onions and potatoes near the end of the cooking time if you like. Remove the vegetables and rabbit from the skillet and add 1 cup grape wine or stock. Stir well and pour over rabbit. If you have been lucky enough to find some wild mushrooms, add them when you do the liquid. This can be thickened with flour if you like.

Hasenpfeffer

One rabbit cleaned and cut into serving pieces. Place in marinade made of equal parts water and vinegar, 3 tablespoons sugar, 1 teaspoon salt that had been boiled together and cooled. Place in a glass or ceramic bowl, add 10 whole cloves and 2 whole bay leaves. Marinate this for two days, turning it several times. Drain and fry in butter to brown. Reduce heat and add 1 cup marinate, cover and simmer 1 hour. Add more marinade or white wine, if necessary to keep it from boiling dry. Add one large chopped onion and continue to simmer until tender . Make a thickening of 3 tablespoons of flour and 1/4 cup water, stir in and cook until it thickens. Stir in 1/2 cup sour cream (heat but do not boil). Remove from heat and serve.

Brunswick Stew

Clean and cut up the rabbit. Let it set in cold water overnight. Place in 4 quarts of water with 1 tablespoon salt. Let this simmer for 1 hour then add everything except tomatoes. Simmer 1 more hour.

1 large onion, chopped	1/2 cup sliced okra (optional)
2 cups fresh lima beans	2 cups corn
2 cups diced potatoes	1 4x4 piece of salt pork
1 tablespoon sugar	1 tablespoon savory
1 quart or 4 cups canned tomatoes	

Bring this back to a boil then put in the tomatoes, heat again and place on just warm heat until finished. Bring heat back to hot. Take 1/2 cup butter and cut into 1/2 cup flour. Add to the pot. Place on lid and cook, boiling 20 minutes. Supper is ready. Serve with a nice crusty bread. This was made on the wood cook stove and was started after morning chores. Then it was set on the back of the stove to keep hot and mingle the flavors. Then it was finished for supper. This was made when a very mature and tough rabbit was butchered. It is equally good with tame or wild rabbit. Chicken and squirrel can be used instead of rabbit. If you don't want the added fat of the salt pork, omit it. Today, when everyone is cutting out fat and our tastes are adjusting, it is okay. You will have enough fat in the butter, but you will need to adjust the salt to your taste.

Squirrel can be used in most any recipe that rabbit can. I know some folk can't think of eating a squirrel but when I was growing up, they were utilized very much. My Dad liked squirrel and in September, he would start hunting. It did not make any difference to him if it was season or not. They were his squirrels and he needed them. The spring chickens were all eaten up and you can't butcher the hogs until cold weather. If the hunting day was not good and he got just one squirrel, we ate it creamed on hot biscuits.

You could stretch that one squirrel to feed all five of us. If it was a good hunting day and he got 3 to 5, they were fried or we had pot pie. Remember this was back in the 30s. We didn't have a refrigerator or freezer, just a cold cellar. Also, laws had not been made to protect our game. When we butchered the hogs, the game animals were all safe until next year. Nothing was wasted; it was used and needed. Today, it is all different. We really never ate that much meat. Certainly not every day. Usually meat was used mostly as a seasoning.

Creamed Squirrel

The animals of how ever many, usually one or two, was cleaned and soaked overnight, at least left to chill out. They were then cooked in salt water until tender, removed from the broth and all bones removed. Back into the pot with a chunk of good cow butter and put to boil. A bit of milk and flour was stirred together, making sure there was no lumps, and then slowly stirred in. The seasoning of salt and pepper was adjusted. This was served over biscuits (see recipe below). You can also use toast.

Anna Lee's Skillet Biscuits

On an electric skillet, set temperature at 340 degrees. Take 2 cups self-rising flour and place in a mixing bowl. Make a hole in the center. Place in this 3/4 cup milk and 1/4 cup corn oil. Mix all well, but don't beat it too much. Into the preheated skillet, drop the dough in 9 equal portions. Cover with the lid and don't peek for 15 minutes. With spatula, turn and continue baking about 10 more minutes. Turn down the temperature to 150 degrees. Leave the lid on until served.

Soft Drop Dumplings

Use the same recipe, but drop the dough in broth, creamed meats, vegetables or fruit for dumplings. Have pan boiling, drop in the dough, cover and cook 20 minutes. Do not lift the lid before 20 minutes.

Squirrel Pot Pie

My Mother prepared the squirrel pieces by frying the young pieces until tender. If there was a big old one, it had to be parboiled then fried. She placed these in a well buttered baking 9x12 pan, sprinkled on salt and lots of pepper and add 2 cups of water. On top of this she put biscuit dough. She cut the dough in strips and placed it lattice style. The wood stove was fired up and ready. The potpie was baked and supper was ready. The supper hour was always the same and Dad knew it. At five o'clock, he was in from the field and Mom knew he'd be hungry so she'd have supper ready.

I do my pot pie differently, simply because I like it better. I keep the squirrel in the refrigerator or freezer till I have enough, usually four. I then cook them in a bit of salt water, butter and chopped onion. When tender, I remove the bones, add the flour and water for thickening. In another pan, I have cooked together onion, chopped celery and sliced carrots. They go in with the creamed squirrel. I pour this into a prepared baking pan, sprinkle on some peas and black pepper. I then make a drop biscuit and drop large spoonfuls on top of the meat and vegetables. Baking this at 375 degrees, these biscuits are done in about 30 minutes. This supper is made at least once each Fall, enjoyed and brings back all those childhood memories.

Raccoon

The meat is very dark and strong in flavor. All fat needs to be removed as well as the scent glands. The animal is covered with fat that extends into the meat. Rinse the animal in vinegar water and wipe dry. Place in the freezer and nearly freeze it to get to the fat. It will be easier to remove this way. Most cooks like to parboil a coon and discard the water, then prepare the meat. Folks use all kinds of things in the parboil water like soda, vinegar, hot pepper, salt and some swear by using black pepper. So, use whatever you like. Remove coon from the parboil and wash in warm water. Return coon to a cooking pot, add salt and water. Cook till just fork tender. Remove and place in a prepared roaster with lid. Bake till tender. Uncover and place precooked sweet potatoes around and continue to cook till browned or, if you prefer, dressing can be made to accompany this.

O'Possum

Though I have never eaten a possum, I know folks who have. The carcass and preparing is like coon, but smaller in size. It is also usually served with sweet potatoes. When having guests for dinner, my son's favorite phrase, when asked what was for supper, was "Possum Pie." Well, usually one or all of our guests would turn green. He always got a hearty laugh and some times waited till we sat down to eat before he confessed it was a joke. Sometimes, he embarrassed me to no end, but it was always the same, no matter if I wanted him to say that or not. One day, I came across a recipe for "Possum Pie." I don't know where it came from or what produced it, but from then on, we did have "Possum Pie" and he really wasn't lying after all. I'm, going to include it here just in case you need to make up a "Possum Pie."

"Possum Pie"

Have on hand 2 cups of cookie crumbs or dry stale cake pieces and combine with 1 cup chopped hickory or pecan nuts. Beat 3 egg whites and gradually add 3/4 white sugar. Beat until stiff. Fold in the crumbs and nuts. Pour into a well greased pie pan and bake 350 degrees for about 45 minutes. Cool. Top with whipped topping and garnish with fruit or berries. If all went well in preparation, you now have your very own "Possum Pie" and I hope you'll have as much fun with it as we did.

You Can, Too, Eat Skunk

In days past, I'm most sure skunk, or more commonly called, Pole Cat, was eaten. Most assuredly the fat was used by the early settlers. Bear fat was the most used fat in herbal medicine but by the time my Grandmother arrived in this area, all the bear was gone, so they used the skunk grease. Trapping was a Winter business and when an exceptionally fit skunk was caught, it was carefully skinned and taken to the house, so the fat could be rendered out. This fat was used to waterproof leather and made into an ointment for year-round use. If the skunk was carefully skinned, so none of the fur ever touched the meat and the scent bag was removed intact, it was nearly odorless. It never smelled like a skunk and it was so much used, for instance, as a base for medicine ointments.

One night, after supper, Grandma needed to cook this skunk, so she placed it in a pan of water to cook on the wood stove, as the final fire burned down. There was no need to look about it, so it just set there cooking. When it came bedtime, she went to bed. In the morning she would remove the fat, fry out the water and keep till it was needed.

As was the winter custom for the men folk, they went night hunting. They never made it plain if they were hunting animals with two or four legs, but a night hunting they would go, especially the young men. This quite often consisted of taking your dog and going to a high hill, building a fire, sometimes roasting chestnuts or potatoes in

the ashes. Usually a jug of moonshine, wine or home brew was carried along. They would sit around the fire swapping tales, eating and drinking. They could listen to the dogs barking, treed or running. It probably depended on how big the jug was if they would go to capture the animal the dogs had found.

Well, this particular night, they must have forgotten to take enough food or was just plain hungry. It has never been quite clear. When those two came in from night hunting here was this nice pot of meat all cooked, smelling so good and even hot. One got out the bread and butter; the other got the plates and silverware. They proceeded to eat Grandma's Pole Cat! Apparently, it was good because they ate it all. When Grandma got up in the morning, nothing was left but the bones. She was quite surprised at that. She never thought about anyone eating that skunk. When the two Grandson's arrived for breakfast and were face to face with the evidence, they admitted to having eaten the meat in the pot. Much to the young men's dismay, they had eaten a skunk. Grandma was not very amused but it was a good joke and is still related at family gatherings and has been for many years. I never think of those two without remembering this incident. They are both gone now, but remember, you can, too, eat a skunk.

Woodchuck was harvested for food as well as to rid the plade of those vegetative eating animals. They make extensive borrows in the best meadows, and, if you or one of your animals steped into a concealed hole, a broken leg was usually the result. No one could afford to lose a cow or horse to this, and if the farmer broke his/her leg, crops could not be planted or harvested or other essential work performed. So, it was important to keep the woodchuck under control. The young is the best eating before they have layered on their winter fat. In days gone by, many a country kid had a pet woodchuck more commonly known as a groundhog--sometimes as a whistle pig because when frightened, they let out a loud whistle as they disappeared down their hole. It is no longer legal to keep wild animals.

When preparing, as with all small game animals, watch out for the scent glands. They are kernel looking, somewhat like fat, under the front legs, thighs, between the shoulder blades and down the back. Carefully remove these whole for the best flavored meat. Remove any fat you can. I like to soak this meat over night in vinegar water, about 1/4 cup to a gallon of water. Some folks parboil before cooking but I don't. If you end up with an old animal, you probably will want to parboil, especially if this is your first try with this meat. Any old animal I have ever cooked was just cooked in water with salt, pepper and an onion. Cook till meat is very tender and will fall from the bones. This was then mixed with BBQ sauce for sandwiches.

Wild Meat BBQ Sauce

1 cup chopped onion
2 cups celery finely chopped
Olive oil to fry
8 ounces tomatoes
2 teaspoons mustard
2 tablespoons honey
1/2 cup water
2 tablespoons vinegar
1/4 teaspoon allspice
2 tablespoons chili powder or to taste
Zest and juice of one lemon
Salt, black pepper and hot sauce to taste
1-2 tablespoons Liquid Smoke or to taste
1-4 cloves garlic minced (amount you desire) or
1/2 cup wild onion tops finely chopped

Saute the celery, add the onions. Cook till limp but not brown. Add the other ingredients in order given. Cook slowly - simmering for 4 hours - stir now and again. This can be used either hot or cold. Most any meat will make BBQ. I use this often with the woodchuck and bear for sandwiches. Place meat in the BBQ sauce and just heat, but don't boil. It is equally good on ribs after they are cooked. Using it cold, it goes well with hamburgers and cold turkey sandwiches.

Pan-Fried Woodchuck

After soaking all night, check again for the little kernels, making sure not to miss any, and cut the carcass into serving pieces. Dust with flour and brown on both sides each piece in some sort of fat or oil. Drain off any excess fat from the skillet. Add a cup of water and very slowly cook till tender. I prefer to use my cast iron skillet for this. Check to see if more water needs to be added. Sprinkle with salt and pepper. You can remove the meat to a serving platter and make gravy from the skillet drippings. Serve up with a bowl of mashed potatoes, cole slaw and any other vegetable that may be ready in the garden. This is an early Summer meal and the woodchuck was not harvested after that.

Woodchuck Pot Pie

Follow recipe for the BBQ woodchuck, but hold the BBQ sauce. After removing from the bone, place meat in a baking pan. Cook up a chopped onion, stalk of chopped celery, some garden peas and carrots in a bit of salted water and add 1/4 cup margarine or butter. Thicken the water and vegetables with a bit of flour. Pour this vegetable mix over the meat and cover with biscuit dough. Bake at 375 degrees about 20 to 30 minutes or until biscuits are done. Add a salad. . . supper is ready.

Creamed Woodchuck

Follow cooking instructions for BBQ, but leave out the BBQ sauce. Mix 1/4 cup flour and 1 cup milk. Cook with the meat and serve over toast or biscuits.

Beaver

Not having beaver roaming around while I was growing up, I never ate one or knew of anyone eating one. Today, it's a different story. We have a man-made lake close by and each Fall a pair of beaver move in and each year they are removed. Well, one year the job fell to my son. He caught the first one and dressed it out. The meat was nice and red, like beef. He left it hanging and came in for dinner asking all those questions about how do you eat or do you eat a beaver. I went to my books and could find nothing on preparing a beaver or if anyone ever ate one. A coon dog came along and took the beaver so no way to try now. Before I could get to a library or find out about beavers, he caught the other one. We decided it was clean and ate vegetative food and it looked awful good. He finished skinning out the creature and sliced off some pieces. He came into my kitchen with words like this: "Fry this for my dinner." There was no cooling out or soaking. I just got out a skillet, put in some butter and spinkled salt over the skillet bottom. When the skillet was sizzling hot, I put in the nice thin slices, fried it on both sides and served it up for dinner. It was very good, sweet and juicy. He decided we would cook that beaver and it was fit to eat, but when he returned to get it, the coon dog had been back and took it again. We very often have those lost dogs a few days and I guess he liked beaver as much as we did. I have never had another beaver to cook or to develop recipes for. I have researched and found recipes for it and it's supposed to be like muskrat but I have never cooked that either. So, I'll leave this up to you.

Fowl of the Land and Water

Wild birds come from the very small, each being one serving, to the largest such as turkey or geese, where you will have leftovers. Each presents its own challenge. Sometimes the hunt will only provide one bird but there are several to feed. In that case, it's usually made into soup or creamed and served over toast.

Wild Turkey

Wild turkey seem to me to be the most challenging of the wild fowl. First, it is usually old and tough, without an ounce of fat on it. If you try to cook it like the conventional bird, it will be something akin to eating cooked cardboard. You must add fat and cook with moist heat. It can be boiled easily and used in soups, salads, pot pies or creamed. If you must roast it whole, here is how.

After cleaning, put giblets on to cook with an onion. These should be cooked slowly with just a simmer. Use this cooking broth for gravy with the giblets chopped. The turkey should be rubbed inside and out with salt and let set overnight. When ready to roast, make meat balls from ground pork (see recipe below) and stuff the bird. Wrap the legs with buttered grape leaves or cloth and pat a bit of the pork mixture on the breast. Place all in a plastic roasting bag and roast slowly, 350 degrees, for about 4 hours or until tender. A nice turkey soup can be made from the leftovers and the bones. Recipe follows.

Roasted Turkey Ball

We start here with a turkey that has been plucked and gutted. Place in cold water to cool. Cut off the tail and wings close to the body and cut around each leg at the bottom to loosen the skin. Cut through the skin and the flesh. Be careful not to tear the skin and work slowly till the skin is removed. Slice off the meat and place with the skin in the refrigerator till morning to finish cooling. Place the wings, neck, giblets and bones in a big stock pot and cover with water. Add 1 large carrot, one onion and 2 stalks of celery. Season with three leaves of sage, salt and pepper. Gently boil till all is tender. If you time this as long as it takes for the gizzard to be tender it will be as long as it takes for your turkey ball to be tender. The age of the turkey will dictate this. Remove the meat from the bones reserving the giblets for your dressing. Make gravy from the broth. You will have left a basic soup stock for another day. You can add rice or noodles for a soup. Do add your bones to the soup pot. In the morning place turkey meat in a food processor with some pork and grind. Add at least 6 egg whites, 1 teaspoon Oriental Five Spices, salt and pepper. Grind to mix. The amount of pork you use will depend on the size of the bird, about 2 pork chops will do for a small bird. A little or a lot of pork is up to you, but not more than 1/2 the weight of the turkey. Work this ground meat into a ball and lay in the center of the skin. Gather up the skin over the meat. Sew or skewer the skin in place and remove before serving. Place the meat in a baking bag and tie shut. Roast at 350 degrees till done, about 4 hours for a young turkey, or time the gizzard to be sure.

Make dressing and cook sweet potatoes. When turkey is tender, remove it from the bag and, on a glass baking dish, arrange the dressing around it. Place the sweet potatoes over the dressing. Return to the oven to brown. I usually use the Chestnut dressing but your favorite dressing can be used. I also cook my sweet potatoes by just scrubbing and either baking or boiling till just tender.

Since I have all those egg yolks left, I will make a cake with this dinner. You must use all those egg whites as that's the glue that holds it together. Since I don't know the size of your turkey, you will need to use your own judgment. I just use whatever amount of egg whites as the cake calls for yolks. It's better to have a little more than not enough. I like Waldorf salad, 3 kinds of pickles / relish and my grape ketchup for this dinner. This is a dinner you will labor over for most of two days, but I bet ya' it will never be forgotten and the leftovers should give you a few days out of the kitchen. What a beautiful sandwich this makes.

Pork Balls Stuffing

1 pounds ground pork	1 tablespoon dry sage
1 tablespoon salt	1 tablespoon pepper
1 tablespoon hot sauce	1 egg
2 cups bread crumbs, more or less	

Mix this all together the night before for the flavors to mingle. Fill cavity with the balls and close opening. Use enough bread crumbs to extend the sausage till you have enough. If bird is small, you may need less. The amount of bread crumbs is not important like the seasoning is. You need this pork to add fat and moisture to the bird. They can be used as an appetizer or served with the bird.

Wild Turkey Soup

After dinner, remove the meat from the bones and put bones on to boil. Add a cup each of chopped onion, carrots and celery. Simmer slowly till vegetables are done and remove the bones. You can add rice, noodles or dumplings if you like. I usually make spazel. This is an old recipe invented before we could buy ready-made noodles. It's worth the effort.

Spazel

1 cup flour 2 beaten eggs
Sprinkle of salt, pepper, nutmeg

Mix this all together with just enough water (about 1/4 cup) to make a soft ball of batter. Let rest till you get the broth to a full rolling boil. Rub the dough through a spazler or through the inside of a grater (the 4-sided kind used to grate vegetables.) Place dough inside and push through holes into the broth. Cover and let boil 20 minutes. The soup is ready to serve.

These spazels are good in most any soup or can be boiled in plain water, drained and then fried. This way they are served as a side dish. Most often at my house, they are served this way with a mess of turnips.

Turkey Pot Pie

3 cups diced leftover turkey
1 tablespoon salt
1 cup celery, grated
1 cup carrot, grated
1 cup broth
1 cup onion, chopped
1 cup peas
1 tablespoon butter

Cook all together till the vegetables are tender. Mix flour-water paste. Stir in the flour-water paste till thickened. Pour into a casserole dish, cover with your favorite biscuit dough. Sprinkle the dough with coarsely ground pepper. Bake in 375 degrees oven about 30 minutes or until browned and bubbly. Serves six.

Turkey Jerky

1 cup water	3 tablespoons olive oil
1 tablespoon ginger	2-3 tablespoons salt
3 tablespoons vinegar or white wine	

Strip meat from the bones in thin strips. Put wings, neck, giblets and bones on to cook for soup. Marinate the meat for 24 hours, stirring often. Dry in 150 degree oven till dry but not brittle. You can vary the seasonings any way you like. If you like a smoky flavor, add Liquid Smoke.

Pheasant

A young pheasant that has been eating a good diet can be fried just like chicken. However, that is usually not the case. The older and tougher birds will require moist heat but usually not much fat. They can be rubbed with salted butter for roasting and basted with more butter during the roasting time. You can place on salt pork if you don't care to baste. Fill with your favorite dressing and place, breast-up, in roaster. Cover and bake at 350 degrees about two hours. If the leg joint will move easily, it's done; if not, cook a bit longer. You do not want to fork-test for tenderness as this lets all the nice juices escape. Remove cover the last 15 minutes to brown. Let set to rest for 15-30 minutes after removing from the oven or while you make the gravy and get everything else on the table.

A very old bird can be cut into sections and partially cooked in a skillet by browning. Add sauerkraut and cover and cook slowly till tender. You may want to just boil and use bird for soup or have it creamed over toast or biscuits. Cook the bird in salt water with a chopped onion. Cool. Remove meat from the bones and return to the broth. Make a thickening of flour and milk. Stir in and cook till thickened.

Wild Duck

There are basically two kinds of wild ducks--ones living mostly from land foods and ones living mostly on water foods. The latter will usually taste very fishy. This is helped by parboiling with the cavity stuffed with carrots, drained, then stuffed and baked. Some always rub the duck of either kind with baking soda and let set overnight, washing well and draining before proceeding to roast. A wild rice stuffing is especially nice with duck, proceed with following cooking guide, but if you have an old one, stuff it with sauerkraut.

Baked Wild Duck with Rice

Soak 1 cup wild rice overnight. Rub the duck inside and out with salt, pepper and butter. Mix wild rice with 1 cup chopped celery and fill the cavity. If the duck is not fat, lay a piece or two of salt pork over the legs and breast. Roast duck at 400 degrees for 50-60 minutes, then reduce heat to 350 degrees, cover and continue to roast for about 3-4 hours. This will depend on the age of the bird. Uncover to brown before serving. I like a tomato preserve with this.

Tomato Preserve

Two pounds yellow or red tomatoes, peeled and sliced. Layer in cooker with three cups of sugar and 1 lemon sliced very thin. Cook slowly till thickened. Makes two pints.

Wild Goose

I have only had a hand in cooking a wild goose twice. I did not like what I came out with, so I won't cover it here. We did not have a season on geese in my area until recently so my chance of having one has always been slim to none. So you are on your own here.

Small Game Birds

In cooking quail, grouse, and other small game birds, you use about the same technique as you do with pheasant. Plan on having one bird per person.

Baked Quail or Grouse / Small Birds

Six quail or grouse sprinkled inside with salt-pepper and thyme. Truss. Brown in a cast iron skillet in butter. Butter six grape leaves and lay on the breast. Add 1 cup dry white wine and continue to cook slowly till tender. You may need to add a bit of water so keep watching the pot so it does not boil dry. Cut the crust from six slices of bread and toast. Lay bird on toast and pour over all liquid left in the pot. Remove the grape leaf. I like to serve this with whipped potatoes and creamed onions.

Creamed Onions

Two large onions peeled and sliced. Cook in a bit of salt water till just about tender, 5 minutes should do it. Add 1 tablespoon butter and a little flour mixed with milk. Adjust the liquid so you have a nice medium sauce. Sprinkle with paprika.

Birds in a Blanket

Take any young and tender bird and rub inside and out with salt, pepper, thyme and butter. Brown well on all sides in a cast iron skillet. Remove to drain while you prepare the bread dough. Either biscuit dough or yeast dough can be used. If I'm taking my birds to a picnic, I use the yeast dough (see below), as it will be cold. Place dough on floured board and roll as thin as possible. Now wrap the dough around and seal the edges. Let rise and continue as if baking just the plain bread. A chicken can be done this way too. Pack up your baked beans, potato salad, stuffed tomatoes, pickles and something to drink and take off to a nice picnic spot.

If I am using the yeast dough (see recipe below), I will serve it hot out of the oven and it will be stuffed with some sort of vegetables or combination of vegetables. Squash with onions or peas and carrots cooked first are often used. A nice cole slaw and a simple dessert are all that is needed for a nice meal.

Yeast Dough for Birds in a Blanket

1 package yeast	4 cups flour
1 1/4 cups warm water	1/4 cup salad oil

Put yeast in 1/4 cup warm water to soften. Mix oil with remaining water in bowl. Let water mixture cool to lukewarm and add the softened yeast. Stir and add about 1 cup of flour. Proceed to add and mix in the remaining flour. Kneed about 10 minutes and put in a warm draft-free area to rise. When raised to double in bulk, work down and roll. Place bird in the center and bring dough up and seal. Place seam-side down in prepared pan. Let rise. Bake at 375 degrees for 30 minutes. If you have dough left over, form into dinner rolls.

You can decorate the top of the dough by making a tiny braid from the scraps or cutting out flowers. Brush the top with milk about 15 minutes before removing from the oven. A few finely chopped herbs can be sprinkled on as well.

Fresh Water Foods

The streams and ponds abound with many different kinds of fishes. One can just eat so much broiled and fried fish. I will try to deal with other ways of cooking, canning and freezing fish plus other water foods.

Freezing--By all accounts it seems the consensus is that submerging your fish in water and freezing is the best way. That is if the fish will fit in a plastic milk box, the most often-used container in this area. Remove from freezer and lay on its side so the water comes out and soon you will have a nearly fresh fish to fix anyway you want.
Canning--This is also a popular way around this area. You must have a pressure canner and the bones will dissolve and they can be used like salmon, tuna or mackerel. Can only in pint jars with no liquid but you can add salt. Clean fish and pack in pint jars, process 100 minutes at 11 pounds at 0-2,000 feet of higher elevation. This is for a dial- type pressure canner. If using the weighted gauge, process the pints 100 minutes at 15 pounds about 1,000 feet. elevation. This is recommended by the U.S. Department of Agriculture Bulletin # 539.

Beer Batter Fish

1 egg, mixed with 1-2 cups of flour and beer used to make a thin batter. Dip in the fish fillets and deep fry.

Fish Sausage

2 1/2 pounds fish fillets, cooked
1/2 pound sausage
1 tablespoon poultry seasoning or thyme
1/4 cup water or fish stock
1/4 cup dry powdered milk
1/4 cup soda crackers, crushed

Grind together the fish, sausage and thyme. Make·hole in the center, add the fish stock and powdered milk then add the soda crackers. Mix all together. If too moist, add a bit more of the cracker crumbs. Form into patties. Flour the cakes and fry now or freeze.

Fish Salad

Do just as you would for any tuna salad using your canned fish.

Pickled Fish

- 2 pounds fillet of fish
- 1 tablespoon sugar
- 1 cup vinegar
- 2 tablespoons coarse black pepper
- 1 tablespoon mixed pickling spices
- 2 tablespoons salt
- 1 cup water
- 1 onion, sliced

Sprinkle the fish pieces with lemon juice and let marinate about 1 hour. Drain and place in pan of water to poach. Place in a sterile glass container. Add sliced onion. Heat vinegar, water, salt and spices (tied in a bag). Pour over the fish. Cool and remove the spice bag. Refrigerate. Serve in a salad or as an appetizer within 1 week.

Fake Shrimp

- 2 pounds of fillet of fish
- 1 can shrimp soup with 1/2 can milk
- 1 cup Ritz crackers
- Butter - Salt - Pepper

Cut the fillets in small rectangle pieces. Place in a buttered casserole. Mix the can of shrimp soup with 1/2 can of milk. Beat with fork to remove the lumps. Pour over the fish fillets. Cover with the cracker crumbs. Dot with butter and sprinkle with salt and pepper. Bake at 350 degrees for 30 minutes.

Fish Cakes

1 tablespoon lemon juice	1 tablespoon chopped scallion
1 tablespoon soy sauce	1 tablespoon black pepper

1 pint of canned fish or 2 cups cooked fish
2 tablespoons mayonnaise

Mix this all together and form into cakes. Dip the fish cakes in 1 beaten egg and roll in bread crumbs. Fry in a bit of oil. Serve.

Fish Chowder

When filleting fish, place the heads and bones in water to cover and cook till done. Remove the bones. Strain off the broth. Return to the pot. To each quart of this stock, add 2 finely chopped potatoes, one carrot and a medium size onion. If making this in dandelion season, I will add 1 cup dandelion buds. Cook till all vegetables are tender.
If you do not have enough stock, the chowder can have milk added to it after the cooking is finished. Heat but don't boil after the milk has been added. Some folks like it better made with the milk. I usually serve up hearty bowls of this with French bread, finger salad food and a rich dessert of rhubarb or strawberry pie.

Fish Loaf

1 pint canned fish	1 tablespoon onion, chopped
1 tablespoon celery chopped	1 tablespoon olive oil
1 egg	1/2 cup bread crumbs
1 cup tomato sauce	Salt and Pepper to taste

Mix all the ingredients together except the tomato sauce. Place in a well greased baking dish. Pour the tomato sauce over top. Bake for 30 minutes in a 350 degree oven.

Poached Fish

Clean the fish as usual. A pair of cotton gloves and thin, sharp knife works best for this. Leave the tail and head attached. Marinate the fish in sherry or white wine several hours, turn several times and sprinkle on salt and pepper so they are well salted. Slit the pocket from the top down next to the ribs. Stuff this pocket with sliced onion and finely minced ginger root. Plan no more than 1 teaspoon minced fresh ginger for each large fish. Place in a pan. Cover and poach. Have the poaching water about 1/2 the way up the fish and poach slowly, turning once. Serve with a butter lemon sauce made with 1 stick of butter and juice of 1 lemon.

Stuffed Baked Fish

Clean fish as usual and with a thin, sharp knife, cut down from the back or top of the fish to make a pocket. Fill this with seasoned bread croutons. Place in baking dish and cover with the following sauce. Bake in preheated 350 degree oven for about 30 minutes or until the fish flakes off easily. The larger the fish the more cooking time. This recipe is for the large fish, not pan sized.

Sauce--Melt 1/2 cup butter in skillet, add one slice onion, 1 cup thinly sliced celery and a bit of fresh parsley. Cook till limp and remove from the pan. Now add 1/2 cup regular flour and lightly brown. Add fish stock to make a gravy.

Return the vegetables and reheat. Pour this over the fish and sprinkle on paprika or coarsely ground black pepper. Place in oven to bake.

Cipco Sauce

- 2 tablespoons olive oil
- 1 garlic clove
- 1 teaspoon black pepper
- 1 tablespoons sugar
- 1 bay leaf
- 1/2 cup white wine
- 2 large cans of whole tomatoes
- 5 pounds fresh water mammal
- 1 cup onion, chopped
- 1/4 cup parsley, chopped
- 1 tablespoon salt
- 1 tablespoon fresh basil
- 1 can tomato paste

Saute in a large 8 quart dutch oven, the onion and garlic till limp. Add the remainder of the ingredients. Simmer for at least 2 hours. A few shakes of hot sauce may be added, if you like. To this pot, add 5 pounds of fresh water mammals of whatever you have such as turtle, frog legs, eel, crayfish and any kind of fresh fish. Cook this slowly till all meat is tender. The more variety the better. Serve over a thin pasta or rice, with a salad and French bread. Serves 10 hungry folks.

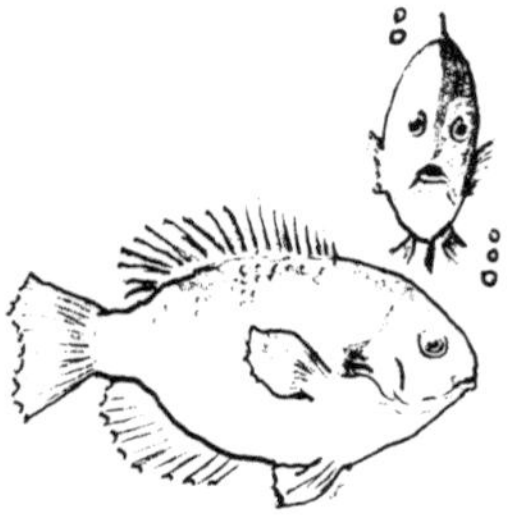

Eel

Eel is a rather strange fish--long and thicker at the head and tapering to the tail, long fins on top and bottom plus broad fins on either side of the head and a mouth full of sharp teeth. The strangest thing is that this fish comes from the ocean and up the fresh water rivers to the small streams. Most fishermen toss them back; however, they are quite good with a sweet moist meat. When caught, wrap and place in the freezer for later use. They should be skinned by ringing around the neck and loosening the skin enough to get a firm grip, pull and the skin will slip right off. Now remove the guts and slice. Slice and dust with a corn bread mix and fry in a bit of butter and sprinkle with salt and pepper.

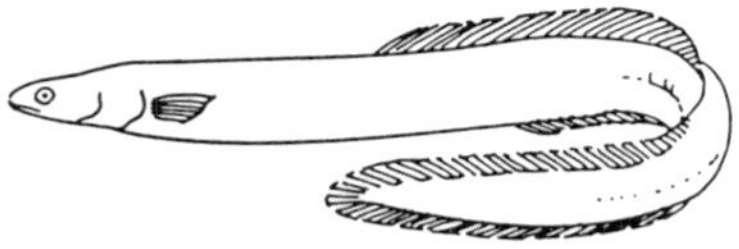

Turtle

A turtle in water is quite docile but out of water and cornered it's a different story. Watch out for bare feet, hands, noisy dogs or other animals, 'cause that turtle will take a bite and won't let go. After you have him caught by whatever means, give him a stick to bite and head for for the chopping block. You can place him in a tub of water to get washed off first, it you like. The turtle will need to be washed in several waters and scrubbed well. This last water I usally use soap and a brush. Some have mud caked on them that must be soaked overnight to remove. When your turtle is clean and head has been removed, scald it with boiling water, then scrape and remove the top layer of the shell. Find where the shell hinges are and cut through these and around enough to get the entrails out. He can now be cooked if small enough to fit any pot you have. If not, the meat will need to be cut from the shell. At this point, put in cold water to cool. The turtle can be rolled in flour, salted and peppered and fried. It is said that a turtle has 7 different tasting parts from beef to chicken. Turtle soup is very good and if you try no other recipe, try it once. I guarantee you will like it.

Turtle Soup

- 1 small cooked turtle, deboned
- 1 cup potatoes, chopped
- 1 cup onion, chopped
- 1 quart of turtle stock
- 1 cup celery, chopped

Cook all together till vegetables are tender. Add enough milk or cream to your taste. Adjust salt and pepper. Serve.

Frog

To me, killing a whole frog just for its legs is ridiculous, but so you will know how, I'll include it here. I have eaten them and they are especially good. First, you have to catch the frog, pierce the brain and cut off the legs and skin. Dust these with flour or corn bread mix. Fry in a bit of butter and sprinkle with salt and pepper. By cooking and de-boning, they can be used in the Cipco, cakes or loaf. Being born just at the end of the Depression, these were free and nourishing foods. In better restaurants, they are on the menu, but I'll just leave them where they are.

BULLFROG

Index